EXPLORE

and

CREATE

Copyright © 1979
PP PARTNER PRESS
Box 124
Livonia, Michigan 48152

Edited by:
Dixie Hibner, B.S. Elementary Education
M.A. Elementary Education

Liz Cromwell, B.A. Elementary Education
M.A. Elementary Education
Certification in Special Education

Illustrated by:
Sue Yagiela Williams

Second Printing May, 1980

ISBN: 0-933212-12-7

Distributed by Gryphon House
3706 Otis Street
P. O. Box 217
Mt. Rainer, Maryland   20822

Dedicated to John Faitel & the ABC's

Table of Contents

ART

Art is an integral part of the education of young children. It cannot be separated from the experiences and skills being developed, during childhood. Indeed, it is useful for the reinforcement of those skills. Through the use of line and color, visual skills are strengthened. Tactile awareness is increased through the exploration of a variety of materials and substances. The child will also expand his experiences, increase his awareness of the environment and improve his self-expression as he explores various forms of the art media.

In addition, art is fun and always a challenge. Art for children must not be competitive. It is an avenue of self-expression and should be regarded as such. Children are expected to put themselves into their work so that each product is different. Art gives every child a chance for success.

This book contains a variety of suggested art activities for young children. It can be used by teachers, parents, babysitters, scout leaders or others who are interested in working with child development.

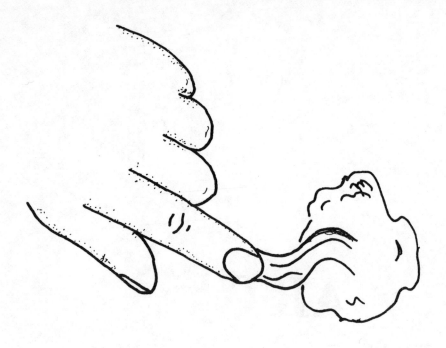

PAINTING

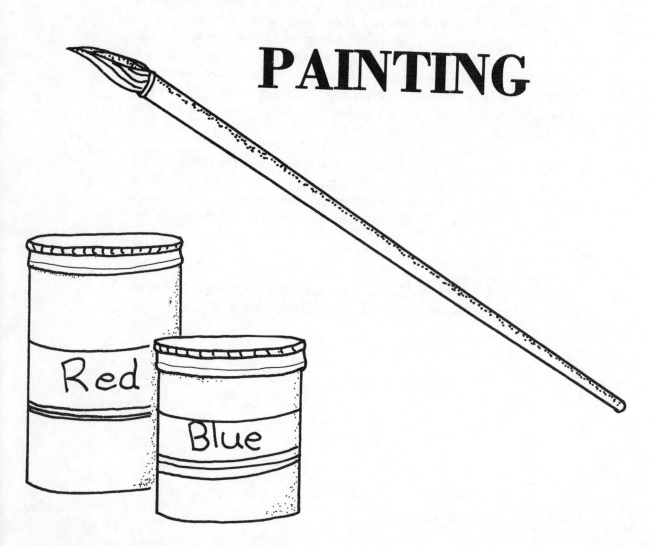

2

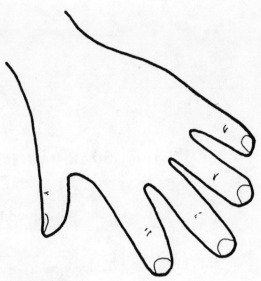

ACTIVITY: **FINGER PAINTING**

OBJECTIVE: Child will increase tactile awareness.

MATERIALS: Shaving cream, cookie sheet or area of a table.

PROCEDURE: — Squirt shaving cream onto the cookie sheet.

— Child "paints" in the shaving cream.

— This is a good way to introduce finger painting. It gets children involved who are reluctant to be "messy." This is also a good way to clean the tables.

VARIATION: Use chocolate pudding for finger painting. If each child has his own cookie sheet he can even lick the "paint" off his fingers.

ACTIVITY: **SOAP PAINT**

OBJECTIVE: Child will expand his experiences in the art media.

MATERIALS: Tempera paint, dry soap flakes, water.

PROCEDURE:
— Mix paint and dry soap flakes; add water only if necessary; mixture should be **very** thick. (Mix with fingers.)

— Children can use this mixture to:

- Make textured paintings
- Coat small bottles or jars to make vases

VARIATION: Finger painting can also be done on shelf-paper cut into large shapes (hearts, balls, triangles, flowers, squares, etc.). This adds variety and can be used to reinforce another concept on which you're working.

ACTIVITY: **COOKIE SHEET PAINTING**

OBJECTIVE: Child will increase tactile awareness.

MATERIALS: Cookie sheet with edges, finger paint, newsprint.

PROCEDURE: — Place one or two colors of finger paint on cookie sheet.

              — Allow child to spread the paint on the cookie sheet.

              — When the painting is completed, carefully place the newsprint over the painting. Press smoothly and lift the print. The finger painting is preserved on paper.

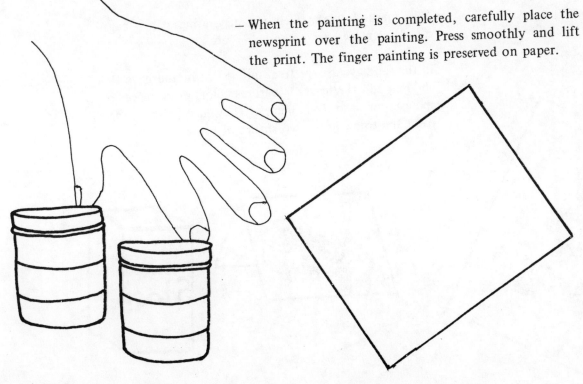

5

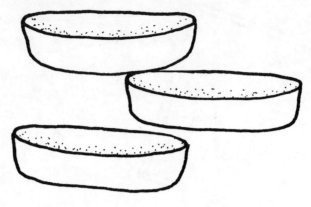

ACTIVITY: **SPONGE PAINTING**

OBJECTIVE: Child will explore self-expression.

MATERIALS: Sponges cut into various shapes, shallow pans of tempera paint, newsprint.

PROCEDURE: Dip the sponge into the paint and blot it several times on the newsprint.

VARIATIONS: — Use a stencil, such as a snowman, and fill in the negative space by sponge painting.

— This method works well for decorating paper bags, cards, valentines, wrapping paper, etc.

— In the fall have a large tree outline drawn and have the children add the leaves in various colors using pieces of sponge cut into leaf shapes. They may also sponge paint the trunk using two shades of brown.

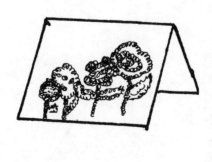

6

ACTIVITY: **STRING PAINTING**

OBJECTIVE: Child will experiment with color and shape duplication.

MATERIALS: String, shallow pans of tempera in two or three colors, paper.

PROCEDURE:
— Fold the paper in half, then open up.

— Dip a length of string into a pan of paint.

— Arrange string on one half of the paper.

— Fold the paper again, and smooth it over the string.

— Open the paper and remove string.

— Repeat, using another color.

VARIATION: The same procedure may be used substituting medicine droppers filled with paint for the string. Dribble the paint on the paper, fold and smooth. Repeat.

7

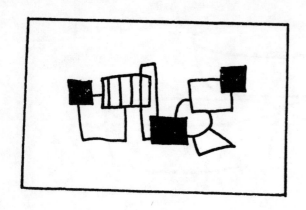

ACTIVITY: **SIMULATED STAINED GLASS**

OBJECTIVE: Child will increase his experiences by exploring the art media.

MATERIALS: Wax crayons, black tempera or watercolor paint, paint brush, paper.

PROCEDURE: — Draw bold heavy lines and shapes with bright colored wax crayons. Be sure to leave spaces of blank paper around the shapes.

— Cover the entire surface with black watercolor paint or watered down tempera. The brightness and clarity of colors are emphasized by black outlines, creating a stained glass window effect.

ACTIVITY: **SQUEEZE BOTTLE ABSTRACTS**

OBJECTIVE: Child will increase his experiences by exploring the art media.

MATERIALS: Plastic squeeze bottles (such as the ones dish detergent comes in), thick white paint, colored chalk, paper.

PROCEDURE: — Let the child squeeze out an abstract design using the plastic bottles filled with white paint.

— Allow the paint to dry thoroughly.

— Fill in the blank areas with colored chalk.

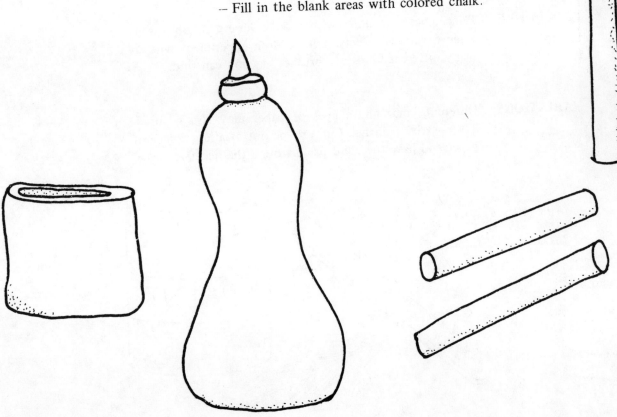

9

ACTIVITY: **EASEL PAINTING OR TABLE PAINTING**

OBJECTIVE: Child will explore various means of self-expression.

MATERIALS: Paint, brushes of various sizes, cotton swabs, feathers, feather dusters, sticks, tooth picks, cotton balls, roll on deodorant bottles filled with paint, toothbrushes, pastry brushes, etc., etc.

PROCEDURE: Painting can be done with a wide variety of objects to achieve various effects. Let children experiment with as many different kinds of "brushes" as you can find.

VARIATIONS: Different kinds and shapes of paper may also be used. Try negative painting. Cut a shape out of a large piece of paper and have the child paint around the negative space.

ACTIVITY: **SALT PAINT**

OBJECTIVE: The child will explore various means of self-expression.

MATERIALS: Tempera paint, liquid starch, salt, brushes, heavy paper or cardboard.

PROCEDURE: — Mix the paint, liquid starch and salt.

— Use the mixture to paint on heavy paper or cardboard. Salt paint is heavier than regular paint.

— When the paint dries, the salt sparkles in the sunlight to create an interesting effect.

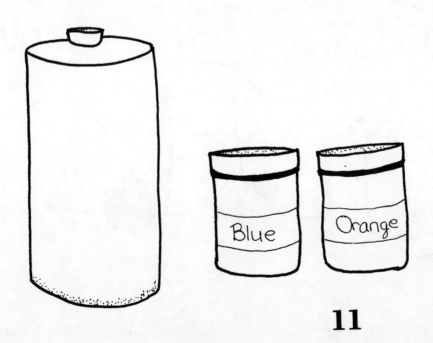

11

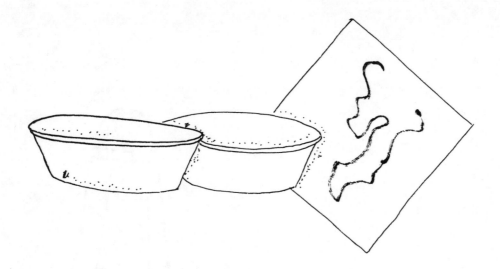

ACTIVITY: **PRINT PAINTING**

OBJECTIVE: The child will increase his experiences by exploring the art media.

MATERIALS: Tempera paint in shallow pans (a sponge in the bottom helps), paper, variety of objects, i.e., potato masher, spools, beads, blocks, toy car with rolling wheels, potatoes cut into shapes, fork, cans, fingers, etc.

PROCEDURE: – Dip an object in the paint and blot it on the paper several times.

              – Repeat with another object or another color.

ACTIVITY: **RUBBER CEMENT DESIGN**

OBJECTIVE: Child will expand his experiences by exploring the art media.

MATERIALS: Rubber cement, paper, paint (watercolor or poster paint).

PROCEDURE: — Dribble rubber cement over the paper in a design.

— Let dry.

— Paint.

— Let dry.

-- Rub off the rubber cement. The design is left.

13

PAPER AND JUNK ART

ACTIVITY: **CRAYON FOIL PRINT**

OBJECTIVE: Child will increase his experiences by experimenting with art media.

MATERIALS: Scrap pieces of crayon, scraping tool (vegetable peeler or grater), aluminum foil, paper, salt shaker, iron, newspapers.

PROCEDURE: — Shave pieces of crayon over newspaper (pinhead size particles).

— Place in clean dry salt shaker.

— Place white paper on newspaper.

— Sprinkle crayon shavings on white paper.

— Place foil over crayon particles.

— Press over foil with moderately hot iron.

— Remove foil and place it on a second sheet and press again.

— Separate foil from paper which has received the printed impression.

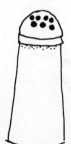

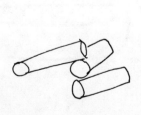

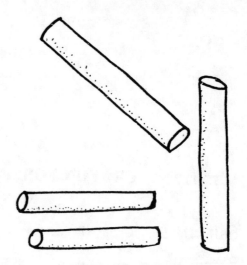

ACTIVITY: **CHALK PAINTING**

OBJECTIVE: Child will explore various means of self-expression.

MATERIALS: Colored chalk, small pans of water, paper.

PROCEDURE: — Let some chalk soak for a few minutes before using it.

   — Dip dry chalk into water.

   — Draw on the paper with wet chalk.

VARIATIONS: Dip the chalk in milk or buttermilk.

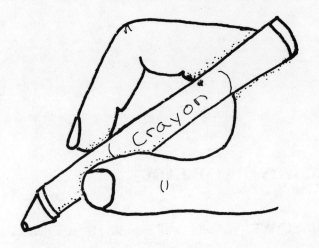

ACTIVITY: **CRAYON RUBBINGS**

OBJECTIVE: Child will expand his experiences by exploring art media.

MATERIALS: Crayons, paper, various objects in the environment (i.e., screen, radiator, sandpaper, leaves, cement, bricks, wall coverings, wood, textured floors, paper clips, etc.).

PROCEDURE: — Place paper over textured object.

— Rub crayon lightly on paper over the object.

— The texture shows through.

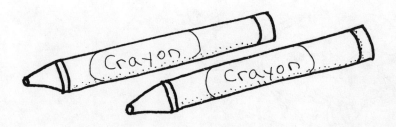

ACTIVITY: **COLLAGE**

OBJECTIVE: Child will expand his experiences by exploring the art media.

MATERIALS: Glue, cardboard or heavy paper, cloth scraps, buttons, seeds, ribbon, macaroni, beans, rice, yarn, twigs, leaves, etc., etc.

PROCEDURE: Glue items of choice on cardboard or heavy paper.

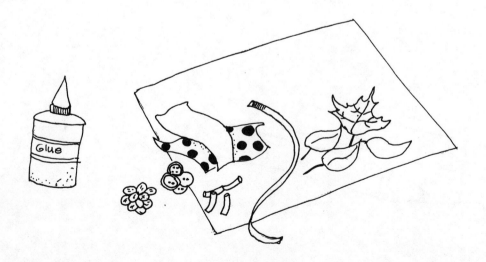

ACTIVITY: **SELF-OUTLINE**

OBJECTIVE: Child will increase self-awareness.

MATERIALS: Child size pieces of paper, crayons, paint.

PROCEDURE:
– Have child lie down on paper.

– Trace around entire body with crayon.

– Sketch in clothing.

– Child will paint or color clothing to match his own and fill in features.

– These can be hung around the room on Parents' night and parents find their own child.

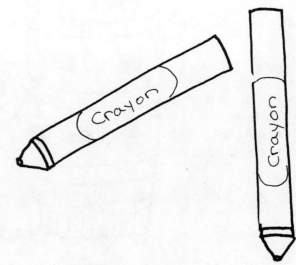

19

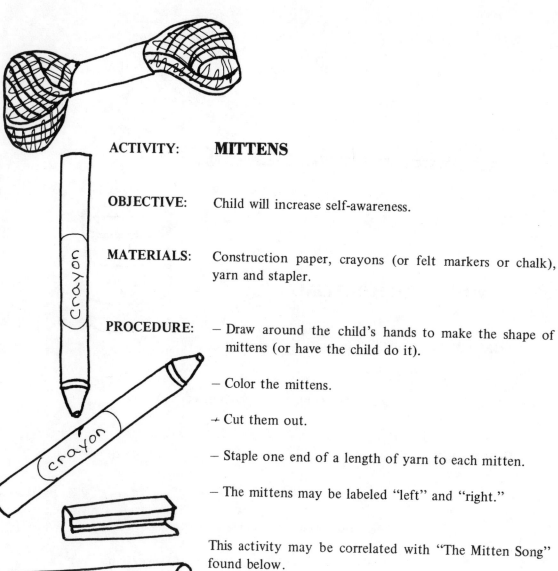

ACTIVITY: **MITTENS**

OBJECTIVE: Child will increase self-awareness.

MATERIALS: Construction paper, crayons (or felt markers or chalk), yarn and stapler.

PROCEDURE: — Draw around the child's hands to make the shape of mittens (or have the child do it).

— Color the mittens.

— Cut them out.

— Staple one end of a length of yarn to each mitten.

— The mittens may be labeled "left" and "right."

This activity may be correlated with "The Mitten Song" found below.

THE MITTEN SONG

Thumbs in the thumb place,
Fingers all together!
This is the song
We sing in mitten weather.

20

ACTIVITY: **GINGERBREAD MEN**

OBJECTIVE: Child will expand his experiences by exploring the art media.

MATERIALS: Brown paper, crayons and round cereal, raisins or chocolate chips.

PROCEDURE: — Outline a large gingerbread man on brown paper.

                 — It may be cut out if desired.

                 — Decorate the gingerbread man using the cereal and crayons.

                 This activity may be used with the story "The Gingerbread Boy."

21

ACTIVITY: **ANIMAL MOBILE**

OBJECTIVE: Child will increase his understanding of his environment.

MATERIALS: Animal templates, pencil, scissors, string, hanger, paste.

PROCEDURE:
— Trace two of each animal to be included, using the templates.

— Cut out the animals.

— Paste the matching animals together, one on each side of a string.

— Tie the string to a hanger.

VARIATIONS: Make mobiles using the following topics.

— Geometric shapes (circle, square, triangle, rectangle).

— Transportation (automobiles, trains, airplanes, trucks).

— Easter (eggs, bunnies, baskets, chicks).

— Valentine's Day (hearts of various sizes).

— Christmas (bells, stars, trees, presents, Santas).

— Fall (leaves of different colors).

ACTIVITY: **PAPER PLATE ANIMALS**

OBJECTIVE: Child will expand his experiences through art.

MATERIALS: White paper plates (try different sizes and shapes), construction paper, paste, crayons or felt markers and scissors.

PROCEDURE: — Cut out head, legs, tail, ears, etc.

— Use crayons or felt markers where desired for effect.

— Paste on the paper plate.

ACTIVITY: **CRAYON ON SANDPAPER**

OBJECTIVE: Child will expand his experiences through art.

MATERIALS: Sandpaper of various textures, old crayons.

PROCEDURE: — Color on sandpaper.

                — Observe and discuss the different effects.

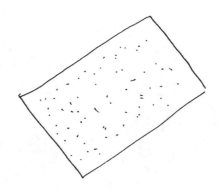

ACTIVITY: **SPRING FLOWERS**

OBJECTIVE: Child will increase his experiences through art.

MATERIALS: Colored paper, tissue paper, paste, scissors and green crayons.

PROCEDURE: — Cut petal shapes from colored paper.

               — Draw stem, leaves and grass on large paper.

               — Paste petals on stem in shape of a flower.

               — Crumple up a small piece of tissue paper and paste in the center of the flower.

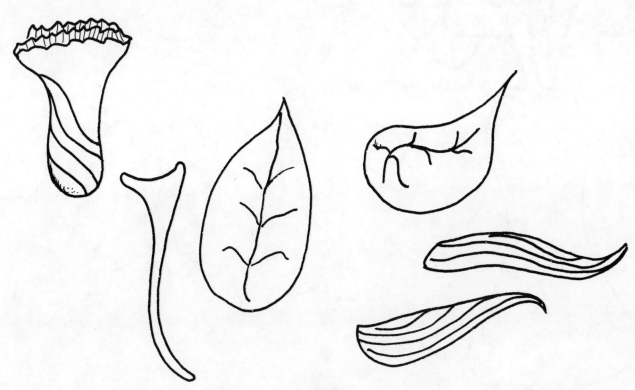

ACTIVITY: **PUSSY WILLOWS**

OBJECTIVE: Child will increase his awareness of the environment.

MATERIALS: Colored paper, wall paper, brown crayons, small bits of cotton, paste and scissors.

PROCEDURE: — Cut a vase shape from wallpaper.

— Paste vase on colored paper.

— Draw stems in vase.

— Paste small bits of cotton on the stems.

Use real pussy willows for comparison.

VARIATIONS: — Use puffed rice cereal in place of cotton bits.

— Use a real vase, and glue cotton bits on real stems.

26

ACTIVITY: **BUTTERFLIES**

OBJECTIVE: Child will expand his experiences by exploring the art media.

MATERIALS: Old crayons, vegetable peeler, waxed paper, newspaper, iron, scissors.

PROCEDURE: — Shave old crayons into bits using the vegetable peeler.

— Place a sheet of waxed paper on newspaper.

— Sprinkle waxed paper with crayon bits.

— Cover with another piece of waxed paper.

— Place another sheet of newspaper over all.

— Press for a few seconds with iron.

— Cut waxed paper into butterfly shape.

— Hang in a window so the light will show off the color.

VARIATION: Cut the waxed paper into flower shapes.

ACTIVITY: **PAPER PLATE TURTLE**

OBJECTIVE: Child will expand his experiences by exploring the art media.

MATERIALS: Paper plates, colored paper, newspaper, paint, paint brush, stapler, scissors.

PROCEDURE: – Cut head, tail and feet from colored paper.

              – Staple between two paper plates.

              – Stuff body slightly with newspaper.

              – Paint the body.

ACTIVITY: **POPCORN TREES**

OBJECTIVE: Child will increase his awareness of the environment.

MATERIALS: Construction paper, crayons or paint, popcorn, glue.

PROCEDURE: – Pop the popcorn. (This can be a classroom activity.)

              – Draw or paint a tree trunk and branches on the
                construction paper.

              – Glue popcorn on the branches to make spring
                blossoms.

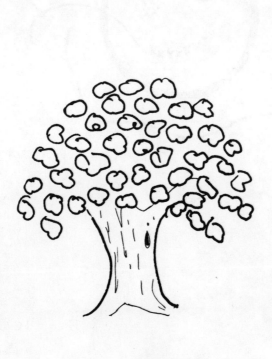

29

ACTIVITY: **SEWING**

OBJECTIVE: Child will develop his fine motor skills.

MATERIALS: Burlap, yarn, yarn needles and embroidery hoop.

PROCEDURE: — Place burlap on embroidery hoop.

   — Thread needle with yarn.

   — Sew a design.

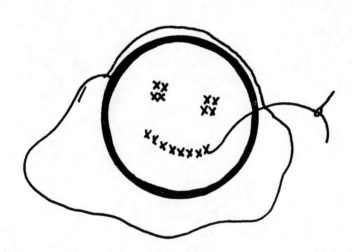

30

ACTIVITY: **PLACEMATS**

OBJECTIVE: Child will expand his experiences through art.

MATERIALS: Waxed paper, newspaper, iron, crayon bits, scraps of colored tissue paper, small flowers, leaves, weeds.

PROCEDURE: — Place a rectangle of waxed paper on newspaper.

               — Arrange other materials on waxed paper to form desired design.

               — Place a rectangle of waxed paper on top.

               — Cover with newspaper.

               — Press with warm iron.

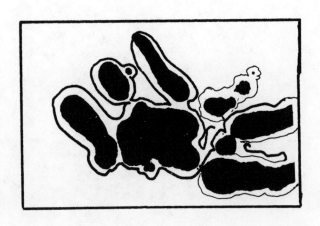

31

ACTIVITY: **WOVEN PLACEMATS**

OBJECTIVE: Child will develop his fine motor skills.

MATERIALS: Construction paper strips, construction paper base, paste.

PROCEDURE: — Prepare the base from 12" x 18" construction paper. Cut vertically in either straight or wavy lines, but not all the way through the paper. Examples:

— Weave the strips through the slits.

— Paste the ends down, so they won't come out.

ACTIVITY: **TREASURE BOX**

OBJECTIVE: Child will expand his experiences through art.

MATERIALS: Cardboard egg carton, paint, brush, small pictures cut from magazines or greeting cards, glue.

PROCEDURE: — Paint the egg carton.

              — Allow to dry.

              — Decorate by gluing on pictures or painting on designs.

A treasure box can be used to store jewelry or other small toys and treasures that children collect.

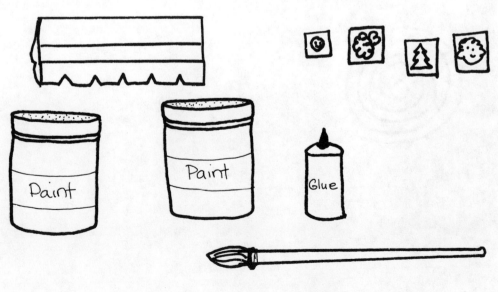

ACTIVITY: **MARGARINE TUB OCTOPUS**

OBJECTIVE: Child will expand his experiences through art.

MATERIALS: Margarine tub, green paper, scissors, felt markers.

PROCEDURE: — Cut legs from a spiral.

                — Make spots on the legs and eyes on the "tub" with a felt marker.

                — Lay the lid, bottom up, on a table.

                — Arrange the legs around the lid.

                — Snap the "tub" onto the lid.

                — Rearrange the legs as necessary.

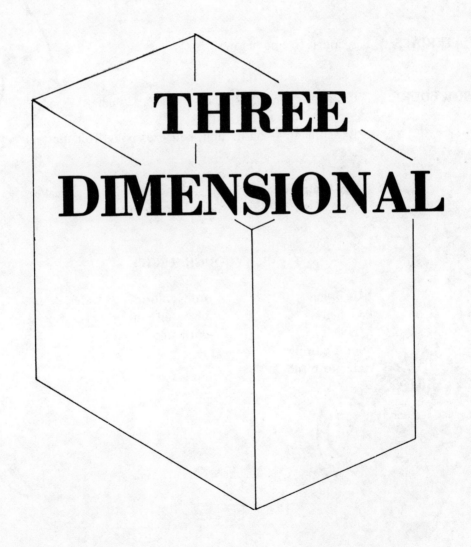

THREE DIMENSIONAL

ACTIVITY: **PLAYDOUGH SCULPTURE**

OBJECTIVE: Child will explore various means of self-expression.

MATERIALS: Playdough (recipe below).

PROCEDURE: — Children may prepare their own playdough.

              — Experiment — push, pull, squeeze, poke, roll, flatten, etc.

              — Try sculpting an object — dish, cup, snakes, pancakes, fruit of various kinds, animals, cars, etc.

PLAYDOUGH RECIPE

2 C. Flour
1 C. Salt
1 T. Oil
Food Coloring
Water to blend

Add coloring to water. Combine all ingredients. Knead until smooth.

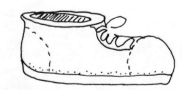

ACTIVITY: **PAPER MACHE SCULPTURE**

OBJECTIVE: Child will explore means of self-expression.

MATERIALS: Newspaper, water, container, paste, paint and brushes.

PROCEDURE: – Tear newspaper into small bits. (Children can do this.
                It's a good fine motor activity.)

              – Soak in water overnight.

              – Squeeze water out.

              – Mix the newspaper with paste that has already been
                mixed according to package directions.

              – Mold into bowls, animals, fruits, etc.

              – Let dry.

              – Paint.

              Another method of using paper mache is found on page
              83.

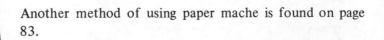

ACTIVITY: **CORNSTARCH CLAY SCULPTURE**

OBJECTIVE: Child will increase tactile awareness.

MATERIALS: Cornstarch Clay (recipe below), paint, paint brush.

PROCEDURE: — Experiment with cornstarch clay — push, pull, poke, roll, flatten, squeeze, etc.

— Try a sculpture.

CORNSTARCH CLAY RECIPE

1 C. Corn Starch ⎫
2 C. Baking Soda ⎭ Mix

Slowly add 1-1/4 C. cold water. Heat, stirring until the consistency of mashed potatoes.

Turn out onto plate and cover with damp cloth. Knead when cool. This clay can be painted when dry.

38

ACTIVITY: **PLASTER SPACE FORMS**

OBJECTIVE: Child will increase his experiences by experimenting with various forms of art media.

MATERIALS: Plaster of Paris, old container for mixing, stick for stirring, yarn and balloons.

PROCEDURE:
— Inflate balloon (tie with string, so it can be hung while drying).

— Mix plaster.

— Saturate length of yarn with plaster.

— Wrap yarn around balloon in decorative manner.

— Allow to harden.

— Puncture balloon.

— Paint if desired.

If you paint the space form before puncturing the balloon, the inside will remain snow white.

39

ACTIVITY: **CARDBOARD BOX TRAIN**

OBJECTIVE: Child will expand his experiences through art.

MATERIALS: Several large cardboard boxes, paint, paint brushes, rope, small sections of dowel.

PROCEDURE: — Paint the boxes. (They should be large enough for a child to fit inside.)

— Punch a hole in the front and back of each "car."

— Tie each end of a length of rope to sections of dowel.

— Insert the dowel into the holes in the "cars" to connect the "train."

— Let the children use the train for imaginative play.

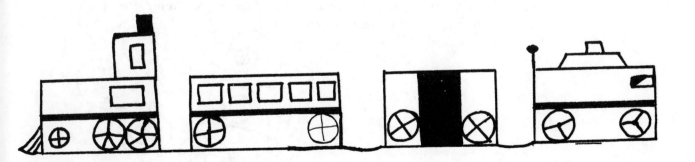

ACTIVITY: **BEAN AND TOOTHPICK SCULPTURE**

OBJECTIVE: Child will expand his experiences by experimenting with art media.

MATERIALS: Beans, tooth picks, bowl of water.

PROCEDURE: — Soak beans in water overnight.

— Make sculpture by inserting tooth picks into beans.

VARIATION: Use miniature marshmallows instead of the beans. Have an extra bowl for tasting.

ACTIVITY: **WIRE SCULPTURE**

OBJECTIVE: Child will explore various means of self-expression.

MATERIALS: Styrofoam, pipe cleaner, soft wire.

PROCEDURE: — Use styrofoam for the base, approximately 3" x 3".

  — Twist and bend the wire or pipe cleaners until they are the desired shape.

  — Insert one end into the base.

ACTIVITY: **YARN MOBILE**

OBJECTIVE: Child will expand his experiences by experimenting with art media.

MATERIALS: Yarn, white glue, waxed paper, shallow pan, string.

PROCEDURE: — Mix glue with a small amount of water in pan.

— Dip yarn in the glue and saturate.

— Arrange yarn on the waxed paper so that there is plenty of overlapping.

— Dry.

— Remove from waxed paper.

— Hang with string.

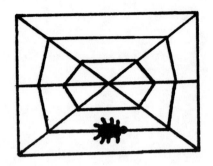

ACTIVITY: **SPIDER WEB**

OBJECTIVE: Child will develop his fine motor skills.

MATERIALS: Yarn, thumb tacks, cardboard.

PROCEDURE: — Arrange thumb tacks on cardboard.

                 — Wrap yarn around thumb tacks to form the spider web.

                 — A spider can be made using construction paper circles and pieces of pipe cleaner.

                 This activity may be used with the nursery rhyme "Little Miss Muffet" or the book "Be Nice to Spiders" by Margaret Bloy Graham.

ACTIVITY: **STUFFED PICTURES**

OBJECTIVE: Child will develop his fine motor skills.

MATERIALS: Butcher paper or brown wrapping paper, paint, newspaper, stapler.

PROCEDURE:
— Cut animal shape from folded paper (so you will have two exactly the same size and shape).

— Paint the animal.

— Staple one side.

— Stuff with crumpled newspaper.

— Staple the other side.

PUPPETS

ACTIVITY: **TONGUE DEPRESSOR PUPPET**

OBJECTIVE: Child will explore various means of self-expression.

MATERIALS: Tongue depressors, felt markers (fine line), scraps of cloth, glue, scissors.

PROCEDURE: — Draw face on tongue depressor with fine line felt marker.

— Cut a piece of material for the clothes and glue onto the puppet.

VARIATION: Magazine pictures of people or faces of the appropriate size may be cut out and glued onto tongue depressors to make puppets.

ACTIVITY: **PAPER PLATE PUPPET**

OBJECTIVE: Child will explore various means of self-expression.

MATERIALS: Paper plates, tongue depressors, felt markers or crayons, construction paper, scissors, glue.

PROCEDURE: — Put a face on the paper plate using either felt markers, crayons or cut pieces of construction paper.

— Construction paper hat, ears and/or hair may be added.

— Glue the paper plate onto a tongue depressor.

ACTIVITY: **PAPER BAG PUPPETS**

OBJECTIVE: Child will explore various means of self-expression.

MATERIALS: Paper lunch bag, crayons, construction paper, paint, yarn, glue, buttons, scissors, etc.

PROCEDURE: — Have some parts precut.

— Have children cut some parts as they assemble the puppet.

— Glue on eyes, nose, mouth and whatever else is desired for each puppet. Bag puppets can take any form — let the children create their own.

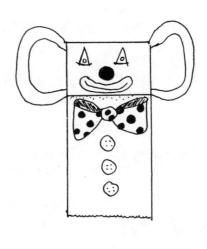

ACTIVITY: **PLAYDOUGH PUPPET**

OBJECTIVE: Child will explore various means of self-expression.

MATERIALS: Playdough, tongue depressor, paint.

PROCEDURE: — Roll the playdough into a ball.

— Form features; pull out nose, poke in eyes, etc.

— Stick in tongue depressor for a handle.

— Paint when completely dry.

PLAYDOUGH RECIPE

| 1/2 C. salt | Mix in a sauce pan and bring |
| 1-1/2 C. water | to a boil. |

2 T. powdered Alum	Add to the above ingredients
2 T. oil	and knead while hot. (Wear
2 C. flour	rubber gloves.) Store in an
	airtight container until ready
	to use.

NOTE: If the playdough is to be used for other purposes, you may want to add a few drops of food coloring before kneading.

49

OTHER KINDS OF PUPPETS

— **Cardboard Roll Puppet** — Long faced puppets can be made on cardboard rolls. Glue on a tongue depressor as a handle.

— **Folded Puppet** — Fold a rectangular piece of construction paper in alternating directions for the body. Make arms and legs in the same manner using strips of construction paper. Add a circle for a head and tape a string on the back of the head.

— **Finger Puppet** — Finger puppets can be made from styrofoam balls, potatoes, apples or anything that can be hollowed out for a finger to be inserted. Simply hollow out the object and decorate it to look like a head.

— **Spool Puppet** — String spools together with elastic, using large spools for the body and small spools for the arms and legs. Thread elastic through a large button at the end of each arm, leg, and head so the elastic won't slip through. Draw a face on the top spool and add yarn for hair if desired.

HOLIDAY

HALLOWEEN

ACTIVITY: **PAPER PLATE PUMPKIN**

OBJECTIVE: Child will develop his fine motor skills.

MATERIALS: Paper plate, orange paint, brush, small pieces of black and green construction paper, paste, scissors.

PROCEDURE: — Paint the paper plate orange.

               — Cut out features for face from black paper.

               — Cut stem from green paper.

               — Paste on features and stem.

ACTIVITY: **PAPER PLATE WITCH**

OBJECTIVE: Child will develop his fine motor skills.

MATERIALS: Paper plate, black construction paper, crayons, paste.

PROCEDURE: — Cut a triangle from black paper for a hat.

               — Cut strips from black paper for hair.

               — Paste onto the paper plate.

               — Draw the features on the plate with crayon.

VARIATION: Make a Jack-O-Lantern with orange paint and paper cutouts.

ACTIVITY: **TISSUE GHOSTS**

OBJECTIVE: Child will develop his fine motor skills.

MATERIALS: White tissues, string, black felt marker.

PROCEDURE: — Crumple one tissue.

            — Wrap it with another tissue.

            — Tie with string.

            — Draw face with felt marker.

            — Hang with the string.

ACTIVITY: **TRIANGLE WITCH**

OBJECTIVE: Child will expand his experiences through art.

MATERIALS: Black paper, light green paper, crayons, scissors, paste.

PROCEDURE: — Cut triangles from black paper for body, arms, legs, hat and hair.

— Cut triangle from green paper for the face.

— Paste together.

— Draw face with the crayon.

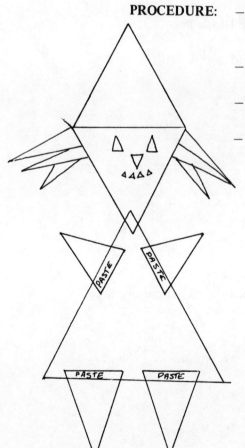

ACTIVITY: **PAPER BAG JACK-O-LANTERN**

OBJECTIVE: Child will develop his fine motor skills.

MATERIALS: Large grocery bag, newspaper, rubber band, paint (orange, black, green).

PROCEDURE: — Crumple newspaper and stuff into the bag.

— Twist the top of the bag and secure with a rubber band.

— Paint the bag orange.

— Paint the face with black paint.

— Paint the stem green.

This is a good group project.

VARIATION: The children can make individual Jack-O-Lanterns using lunch size bags.

THANKSGIVING

ACTIVITY: **HANDPRINT TURKEY**

OBJECTIVE: Child will develop his fine motor skills.

MATERIALS: Paper, crayons.

PROCEDURE: — Trace around hand.

— Add feet and beak.

— Color.

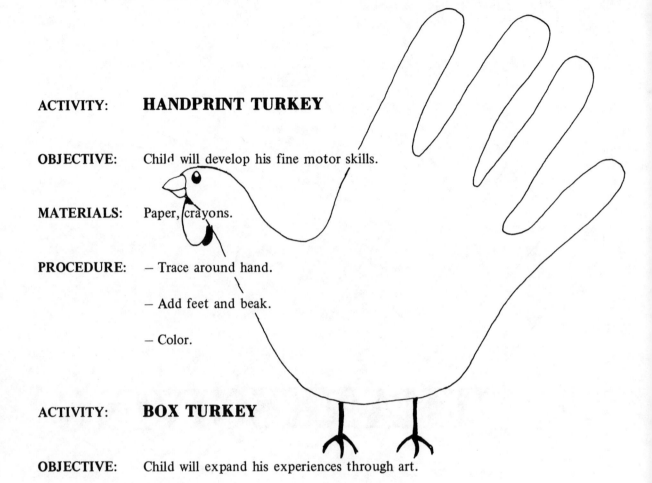

ACTIVITY: **BOX TURKEY**

OBJECTIVE: Child will expand his experiences through art.

MATERIALS: Salt box (or oatmeal box), colored paper, scissors, paste.

PROCEDURE: — Wrap brown paper around the box and paste.

— Cut tail feathers from colored paper and paste on one end of the box.

— Cut head from brown paper and paste on the other end. (Cut into the end of the neck and fold so it will be easier to paste onto the box.)

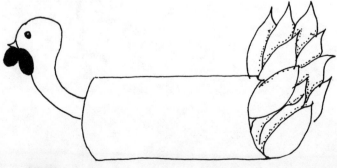

58

ACTIVITY: **INDIAN VEST**

OBJECTIVE: Child will expand his experiences through art.

MATERIALS: Grocery bag, scissors, potato, knife, paint, shallow pan.

PROCEDURE: — Cut vest from the grocery bag. Cut arm holes in the
                   sides. Cut an opening up the front and space for the
                   neck.

                 — Cut the potato in half and carve an Indian design in
                   each half for print painting on the vest.

                 — Dip the potato into shallow pan of paint and press
                   onto the vest.

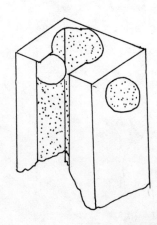

59

ACTIVITY: **INDIAN HEADBAND**

OBJECTIVE: Child will expand his experiences through art.

MATERIALS: Construction paper strips, scissors, stapler.

PROCEDURE: – Children cut feathers from strips of construction paper.

— Each child may cut a few feathers to be a "brave" or a lot of feathers to be a "chief."

— Staple the feathers to a strip of construction paper and adjust to fit the child's head.

The headband may be worn with the Indian vest on the preceding page.

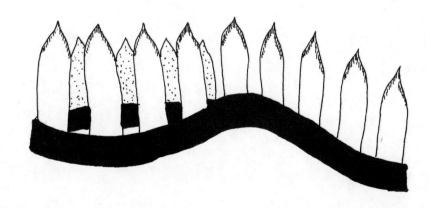

ACTIVITY: **INDIAN DRUM**

OBJECTIVE: Child will expand his experiences through art.

MATERIALS: Oatmeal box, tape, yarn, paint.

PROCEDURE:
– Tie a piece of yarn through the bottom of the box so it can be worn around the neck.

– Tape the lid on the box.

– Paint.

– Decorate with Indian designs.

61

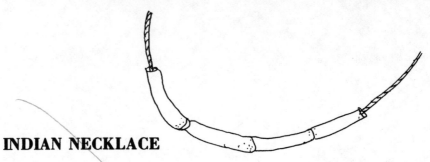

ACTIVITY: **INDIAN NECKLACE**

OBJECTIVE: Child will expand his experiences through art.

MATERIALS: Large macaroni, yarn, tape, food coloring, containers (small plastic bowls), water, cookie sheets.

PROCEDURE: — Mix food coloring and water in container.

— Add the macaroni.

— Stir gently for a short time.

— Remove and place on the cookie sheets to dry.

— Wrap tape around one end of a length of yarn.

— String the macaroni.

— Tie the ends together.

VARIATION: Use a large needle and heavy thread to make a necklace from the following:

pumpkin seeds

lima beans (soak them overnight first)

small pieces of paper

short lengths of straw

playdough beads.

ACTIVITY: **PILGRIM HAT (GIRL'S)**

OBJECTIVE: Child will expand his experiences through art.

MATERIALS: White construction paper (12" x 18"), white yarn, stapler, scissors.

PROCEDURE: — Cut on the lines.

              — Fold on the dotted lines.

              — Staple the back of the hat.

              — Staple a length of yarn on each side so the hat can be tied onto the head.

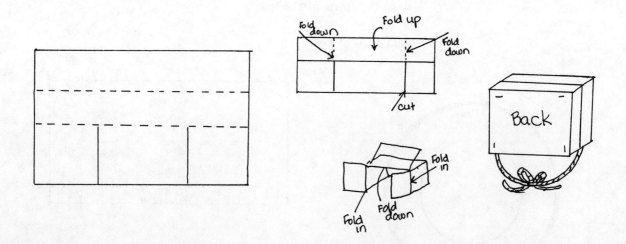

ACTIVITY: **PILGRIM HAT (BOY'S)**

OBJECTIVE: Child will expand his experiences through art.

MATERIALS: Black and yellow construction paper, black yarn, stapler, paste.

PROCEDURE: — Cut a brim large enough to fit on the child's head.

— Cut a strip about 6" to 8" wide and long enough to go around the child's head. (You may need to staple two pieces together.)

— Cut into the edge about 1/2" along one side.

— Form into a cylinder and staple.

— Fold up the cut edges and staple to the brim.

— Cut a buckle from yellow construction paper and paste onto the front of the hat.

— Add yarn to tie.

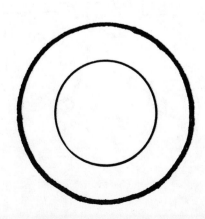
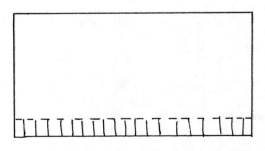

64

CHRISTMAS

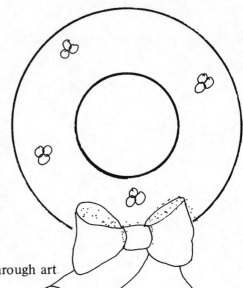

ACTIVITY: **WREATH**

OBJECTIVE: Child will expand his experiences through art.

MATERIALS: Soap flakes, green paint, brush, bowl, water, mixer, paper plate, seeds or buttons, ribbon or crepe paper, glue.

PROCEDURE: — Cut a hole in the center of the paper plate.

— Mix the soap flakes, a little green paint and a little water. (This should be very thick.)

— Spread thickly on the paper plate.

— Press in buttons or seeds.

— Let dry.

— Make a bow from ribbon or crepe paper and glue onto the wreath.

VARIATION: The paper plate base may also be used to make a wreath with tissue paper. Cut small strips of green tissue paper, fold in half, twist the folded end and glue on the paper plate. Repeat until the plate is covered.

66

ACTIVITY: **STAINED GLASS WINDOWS**

OBJECTIVE: Child will increase his awareness of the envrionment.

MATERIALS: Black construction paper, colored cellophane, scissors, tape or stapler.

PROCEDURE: — Cut spaces from the black construction paper.

— Tape or staple the cellophane to the back.

— Hang in a window.

ACTIVITY: **CHRISTMAS CARDS**

OBJECTIVE: Child will expand his experiences through art.

MATERIALS: Paper (white or colored), glitter, glue, crayons or felt markers.

PROCEDURE: — Fold the paper as for a card.

— Color a picture on the front. (Such as a Christmas tree, candle, bell, star, etc.)

— Dribble glue on the picture where glitter is desired.

— Sprinkle with glitter. (Do this over paper so that the excess can be saved and reused.)

— Write a message on the inside of the card.

ACTIVITY: **PAPER PLATE SANTA**

OBJECTIVE: Child will develop his fine motor skills.

MATERIALS: Paper plate, cotton balls, red paper, crayons or felt markers, paste.

PROCEDURE: — Cut a hat from red paper.

— Paste onto the plate.

— Paste on cotton balls for beard and trim of the hat.

— Draw the face.

VARIATION: An angel can be made from a paper plate in a similar fashion. Draw a face on the plate. Glue on yarn for the hair. Bend a pipe cleaner to make the halo.

ACTIVITY: **SPIRAL TREE DECORATION**

OBJECTIVE: Child will develop his fine motor skills.

MATERIALS: Colored paper, scissors, string, glitter, glue.

PROCEDURE: — Draw a spiral line on a piece of paper.

— Cut on the line.

— Dribble on glue.

— Sprinkle glitter on the glue. (Do this over paper so the excess can be saved and reused.)

— Attach string to the center of the spiral and hang on the tree.

ACTIVITY: **SILVER BELLS**

OBJECTIVE: Child will develop his fine motor skills.

MATERIALS: Small paper cup, aluminum foil, pipe cleaner.

PROCEDURE: — Cover the paper cup with aluminum foil.

— Insert a pipe cleaner, making a hook at each end. One hook is to hang the "bell," the other to keep the "bell" on the pipe cleaner.

— Hang on the Christmas tree.

ACTIVITY: **MODELING DOUGH ORNAMENTS**

OBJECTIVE: Child will expand his experiences through art.

MATERIALS: Modeling dough (recipe below), cookie cutters, rolling pin, extra flour, tooth pick, paint, brush.

PROCEDURE: — Roll out the modeling dough like cookie dough.

                — Cut with cookie cutters or cut a free form design.

                — While still soft, punch a hole with a tooth pick near the top.

                — Let dry. (This will take 2 — 3 days.)

                — Paint.

                — Tie a string through the hole.

MODELING DOUGH RECIPE

1-1/2 C. water
2 C. salt
1 C. cornstarch

Mix salt and cornstarch together. Bring water to a boil; remove from heat. Add salt and cornstarch slowly while stirring. Continue to cook over low heat until the dough is hard to stir. Remove from pan. Let cool. Knead. Store in an air tight container.

ACTIVITY: **CHRISTMAS TREE**

OBJECTIVE: Child will develop his fine motor skills.

MATERIALS: Green paper, scissors, stapler, glue, glitter.

PROCEDURE: — Cut paper into rectangles 4-1/2" x 6", or 6" x 9".

— Fold in half the long way.

— Staple on the fold, using two rectangles.

— Fold again and cut from the top of center fold to bottom outside corner.

— Cut slashes into the side of the triangle.

— Unfold.

— Bend the slashes in alternating directions.

— Dribble glue on the edges and sprinkle with glitter.

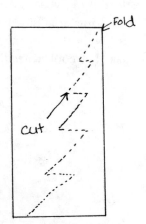

ACTIVITY: **CHRISTMAS TREE MURAL**

OBJECTIVE: Child will expand his experiences through art.

MATERIALS: Large paper, small pieces of paper, felt markers, glitter, glue, scissors, green paint, brushes.

PROCEDURE: — Outline a Christmas tree on the large paper.

                     — Paint the tree. (Children can do this too.)

                     — Cut out ornaments from the small pieces of paper and decorate with felt markers and glitter.

                     — Hang on the tree.

ACTIVITY: **REINDEER PUPPET**

OBJECTIVE: Child will expand his experiences through art.

MATERIALS: Lunch sized paper bag, brown paper, black, and white paper scraps, scissors, glue.

PROCEDURE: — Trace around hands on brown paper, cut out and glue on for antlers.

      — Cut eyes and nose from black paper and glue onto the folded bottom of the bag.

      — Cut spots from white paper and glue onto the side of the bag.

VARIATION: This puppet may be given a red nose and become Rudolph. It could then be used along with the story or record "Rudolph the Red Nosed Reindeer."

ACTIVITY: **WRAPPING PAPER**

OBJECTIVE: Child will expand his experiences through art.

MATERIALS: Potatoes (cut in half), paint, shallow pans, sponges, newsprint or butcher paper.

PROCEDURE: — Carve away part of the surface of the potato leaving a Christmas shape, such as:

— Place a small amount of paint over a sponge in a shallow pan.

— Press the surface of the potato on the paint soaked sponge and then onto the paper.

— Allow time to dry.

— Wrap gift.

VARIATIONS: — Use Christmas cookie cutters in place of potatoes.

— Glue string or yarn onto heavy cardboard in a Christmas shape. Paint the string and then press onto the paper.

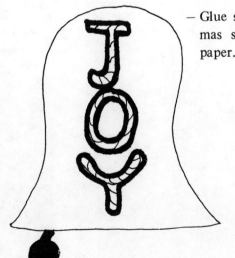

75

VALENTINE'S
DAY

ACTIVITY: **SPONGE PAINTING**

OBJECTIVE: Child will expand his experience through art.

MATERIALS: Sponges cut into heart shapes of varying sizes; red, white, and pink paper; red, white, and pink paint; shallow pans.

PROCEDURE: — Use any combinations of colors of the paint and paper.

— Dip the sponge into the paint.

— Press onto the paper.

ACTIVITY: **HEART PAINTING**

OBJECTIVE: Child will increase his ability to express himself.

MATERIALS: Easel, paint, brushes, newsprint cut into large heart shapes, tape.

PROCEDURE: — Tape the heart shaped paper to the easel.

— Paint.

VARIATION: Use paper from which a heart shape has been cut. The child then paints around the heart shape.

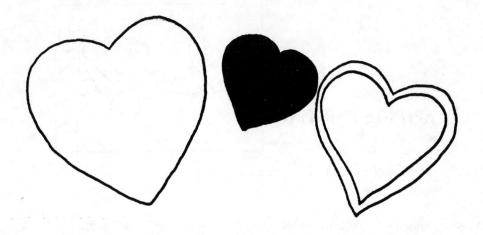

ACTIVITY: **VALENTINE BOX**

OBJECTIVE: Child will expand his experiences through art.

MATERIALS: Shoe box, paint, brushes, colored paper, scissors, glue.

PROCEDURE: — Paint the shoe box.

— Cut heart shapes from folded colored paper.

— Glue onto the box to decorate.

Use the box for a valentine mailbox.

ACTIVITY: **VALENTINES**

OBJECTIVE: Child will increase his ability to express himself.

MATERIALS: 9" x 12" paper; scissors, glue, small pieces of red, pink and white construction paper, paper doilies, foil paper, tissue paper, bits of lace and ribbon, flower pictures cut from magazines, etc.

PROCEDURE: — Fold the 9" x 12" paper in half to form the card.

— Allow the child to create his own valentine using the materials available.

— Write the message dictated by the child on the inside of the card.

ACTIVITY: **HEART COLLAGE**

OBJECTIVE: Child will increase his ability to express himself.

MATERIALS: Paper, hearts cut in varying colors and sizes, glue.

PROCEDURE: Glue hearts on the paper to form objects or designs.

80

EASTER

ACTIVITY: **EASTER BASKET TREE**

OBJECTIVE: Child will expand his experiences through art.

MATERIALS: Tree branch, container of sand, egg shell halves, egg dye, pipe cleaners, Easter "grass", jelly beans, glue.

PROCEDURE: — Secure tree branch in container of sand.

              — Dye the egg shell halves.

              — Attach pipe cleaner with glue for a handle.

              — Put in a little "grass" and a few jelly beans.

ACTIVITY: **PAPER MACHE EGGS**

OBJECTIVE: Child will increase his ability to express himself.

MATERIALS: Newspaper, wheat paste, paint, brushes (some small).

PROCEDURE: — Tear newspaper into small strips.

              — Wad a piece of newspaper into an egg shape.

              — Wet the newspaper strips with wheat paste and wrap
              around the egg shape.

              — Add several layers of paper strips.

              — Let dry.

              — Paint.

Another method of using paper mache is found on page 37.

ACTIVITY: **EASTER BUNNY**

OBJECTIVE: Child will expand his experiences through art.

MATERIALS: Can (vegetable, fruit, etc.), white paper, pink paper, glue, felt marker, pipe cleaners.

PROCEDURE: – Cover the can with white paper.

– Draw face with felt markers.

– Cut ears from white paper and the centers from pink.

– Glue on ears.

– Glue on pipe cleaners for whiskers.

ACTIVITY: **BABY CHICKS**

OBJECTIVE: Child will expand his experiences through art.

MATERIALS: Cotton balls, yellow powdered poster paint, plastic bag, scraps of black and orange paper, egg shell halves, glue.

PROCEDURE: — Place the powdered paint in the plastic bag, add the cotton balls and shake.

— Glue two cotton balls together.

— Glue the cotton balls inside the egg shell half.

— Add eyes and beak cut from the black and orange paper scraps. (Eyes can be made quickly and easily by using a paper punch.)

ACTIVITY: **PAPER LOOP RABBIT**

OBJECTIVE: Child will develop his fine motor skills.

MATERIALS: White paper, scissors, glue, cotton ball.

PROCEDURE: — Cut 3" wide strips from the white paper.

— Form two loops, one large and one small, from the strips.

— Glue together using the large loop for the body, the small one for the head.

— Cut out and glue on ears.

— Glue on a cotton ball for the tail.

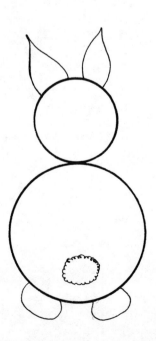

GAMES

Playing games is a natural part of childhood. Children play games primarily because they're fun. What adult doesn't have pleasant memories of games played during childhood?

Playing games is also a means of self-expression, reinforcement for developmental skills and an avenue for social interaction. Games can develop good sportsmanship and many games promote thinking skills as well.

The games included in this book were chosen for use with young children. There are few rules and competition is not stressed. The foremost idea is to have a good time. Children learn more when they enjoy what they're doing.

Have fun with Games!

CLASSROOM GAMES

ON THE BANK, IN THE POND

MATERIALS: A circle representing the pond.

PROCEDURE:

— The children all stand on the outside of the circle representing the pond. They are "on the bank." Inside the circle is "in the pond."

— The teacher (or a designated child) calls out, "In the pond, on the bank," etc., rapidly as the children jump back and forth over the line.

— One instruction may be called several times in succession.

— When someone jumps the wrong way, he must go into the center of the circle.

POLICEMAN

MATERIALS: Place for two children to be removed from the group so they can't see each other.

PROCEDURE: — A child is chosen to be the policeman. He/she then leaves the room.

— Another child is chosen to be lost, and leaves or hides.

— The policeman returns and the children say, "Policeman, policeman, my child is lost! Who is it?"

— The policeman has three guesses to determine which child is missing.

— Choose another policeman and repeat.

DOGGIE, DOGGIE, WHERE'S YOUR BONE?

MATERIALS: An object to represent the bone, such as a small block.

PROCEDURE:
- Children sit in a circle with their hands closed in their lap.

- One child selected as the doggie either leaves the room or sits in the center of the circle with his eyes closed.

- The doggie either returns or opens his eyes as the group chants, "Doggie, doggie, where's your bone? Hurry up and bring it home."

- The doggie has three guesses in which to determine who has the bone.

- Choose a new doggie and repeat.

91

STATUE

MATERIALS: Piano or record player and musical record.

PROCEDURE: — Play the piano or the record while the children go through creative motions to the music.

— Stop the music after a few seconds.

— When the music stops, the children "freeze."

— Repeat.

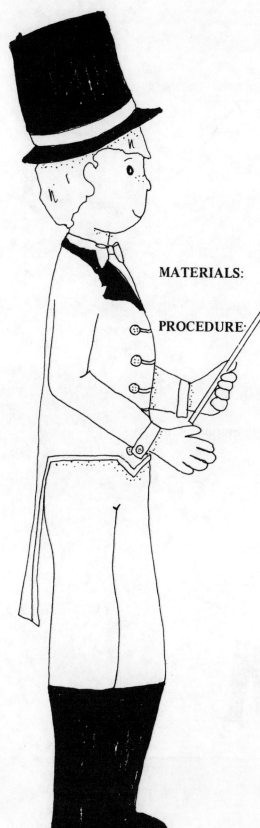

RINGMASTER

MATERIALS: None.

PROCEDURE:

- The children stand in a circle with the ringmaster in the center.

- The ringmaster calls out the name of an animal and the other children move around the circle imitating that animal.

- Change the ringmaster often so that more than one child gets to be the ringmaster.

93

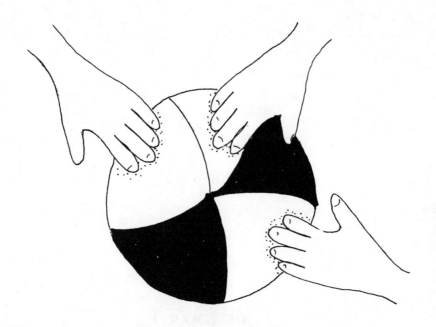

BAT BALL

MATERIALS: Large lightweight ball such as a beach ball.

PROCEDURE: — Children stand in a circle.

— The ball is hit with the hands or arms.

— The children try to keep the ball in motion as long as they can.

NAME BALL

MATERIALS: Large ball.

PROCEDURE: – Children sit in a circle.

– The child with the ball calls out the name of another child and then rolls, bounces or throws the ball to that child.

COMMENT: This game can be used to help children learn the names of others in the group.

FOOT BALL

MATERIALS: Large lightweight ball.

PROCEDURE: – Children sit in a circle.

                  – A ball is rolled into the center of the circle.

                  – The children kick the ball with the bottoms (no toes) of one or two feet.

                  – They try to keep the ball in motion and inside the circle.

GOOD MORNING

MATERIALS: None.

PROCEDURE: – The children sit in a circle with one child walking around the outside.

– This child taps someone on the head and continues walking around the circle.

– The child who was tapped goes around the circle in the opposite direction.

– They meet half way around the circle, shake hands and say, "Good morning."

– They continue around the circle to the vacant space. The last one back becomes "it."

– Repeat.

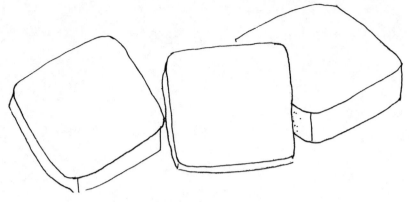

COME WITH ME

MATERIALS: Chairs, pillows or something else to mark each child's spot.

PROCEDURE:
– The children all sit in a circle with one child ("it") standing on the outside of the circle. (If you use chairs, you might turn them so they face out – or leave enough space between them for children to get in and out of the circle.)

– "It" walks around the outside of the circle and taps several children on the head, saying each time, "Come with me."

– Those children who are tapped follow "it" and put their hands on the shoulders of the children in front of them.

– They continue around the circle in this manner until the leader says, "Everybody go home."

– The children all race for the empty spaces.

– One child will be left over, and that child becomes "it."

– Repeat in the same manner.

BELLY LAUGH

MATERIALS: None.

PROCEDURE: — The children lie on the floor on their stomachs. They should form a circle, facing in, so everyone can see everyone else.

— Point to a child and that child says, "Ha."

— That child then points to another child who says, "Ha, ha." This is repeated, adding a "ha" each time until someone laughs.

EXAMPLE: First person: "Ha."

Second person: "Ha, ha."

Third person: "Ha, ha, ha."

Fourth person: "Ha., ha, ha, ha."

Etc.

— When someone laughs, the game is repeated in the same manner.

 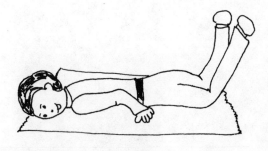

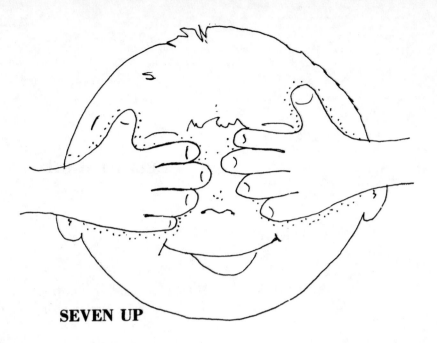

SEVEN UP

MATERIALS: None.

PROCEDURE: — Seven children stand in front of the group. The remainder of the children cover their eyes.

— The seven children each tap another child lightly on the head and return to their position in front of the group.

— Say "Seven-up." The children then uncover their eyes and the seven who were tapped stand up.

— They try to guess who tapped them. If a child guesses correctly, he takes the place of that person in front of the group.

— Repeat.

POSTMAN

MATERIALS: None needed, but you may improvise a postman's hat and mailbag to be worn by the postman.

PROCEDURE: — The children sit in a circle and one child is chosen to be the postman.

— He says, "I have a letter for . . . . .," he then describes someone in the group.

— The children try to guess who the letter is for.

— The child who guesses correctly, gets to be the new postman and the game is repeated in the same manner.

DAVY CROCKETT

MATERIALS: A toy gun.

PROCEDURE: – The children sit in a circle, with one child (Davy Crockett) in the center.

     – There is a gun behind Davy Crockett and he closes his eyes (goes to sleep).

     – Choose someone from the circle to "steal" the gun and hide it behind them.

     – The children then say, "Davy Crockett, wake up! Someone has stolen old Bess!"

     – Davy Crockett opens his eyes and tries to guess (3 guesses) who has the gun.

     – If he doesn't guess correctly in three attempts, the child with the gun gets to be Davy Crockett.

     – If he does guess correctly, he gets to choose a new Davy Crockett.

POOR PUSSY

MATERIALS: None.

PROCEDURE: — Children sit in a circle.

— One child is selected to be the "pussy."

— Pussy crawls up to someone in the circle and says, "Meow."

— That person must pat Pussy's head and say, "Poor Pussy, poor pussy, poor pussy." (3 times.)

— The Pussy tries to make that person laugh.

— If he laughs, he becomes the Pussy. If he doesn't laugh, the original Pussy crawls up to someone else and tries again.

103

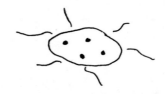

HOT POTATO

MATERIALS: Ball, record player and record.

PROCEDURE: — Have children sit on the floor in a circle.

— Hand the ball to one child.

— Start to play the record.

— The children pass the ball around the circle as rapidly as possible when the music plays.

— When the music stops, the child who is holding the ball is out of the game.

— The game proceeds in this manner until there is only one child left in the game.

COMMENT: If you are working with a large group of children, it may be desirable to divide them into two groups.

THE SNAIL

MATERIALS: None.

PROCEDURE: — The children join hands in a line.

— As they say the verse below, the leader leads them into a spiral on the first verse and back out on the second.

VERSE 1: Hand in hand you see us well,
Creep like a snail into his shell.
Ever nearer, ever nearer.
Ever closer, ever closer.
Very snug indeed you dwell,
Snail within your tiny shell.

VERSE 2: Hand in hand you see us well,
Creep like a snail out of his shell.
Ever farther, ever farther.
Ever wider, ever wider.
Who'd have thought this little shell,
Could have held us all so well.

AROUND AND AROUND

MATERIALS: None.

PROCEDURE: — Children stand in a circle and perform the actions indicated as they say the following:

Around and around in a ring we go.
First we go fast and then we go slow.
We stop and raise our arms high,
Until we almost reach the sky.
We drop our hands and turn around.
We stand in place without a sound.

JACK BE NIMBLE

MATERIALS: Candle and candlestick, or use a block and pretend.

PROCEDURE: — Children sit in a circle with the candlestick in the center.

— The children take turns jumping over the candlestick while they all chant:

Jack be nimble,
Jack be quick,
Jack jump over the candlestick!

— Substitute the child's name for Jack.

EVERYBODY DO THIS

MATERIALS: None.

PROCEDURE: — Children take turns doing some kind of motion for the
others to imitate while all sing:

Everybody do this, do this, do this.
Everybody do this, just like me.

108

OUTDOOR OR GYM GAMES

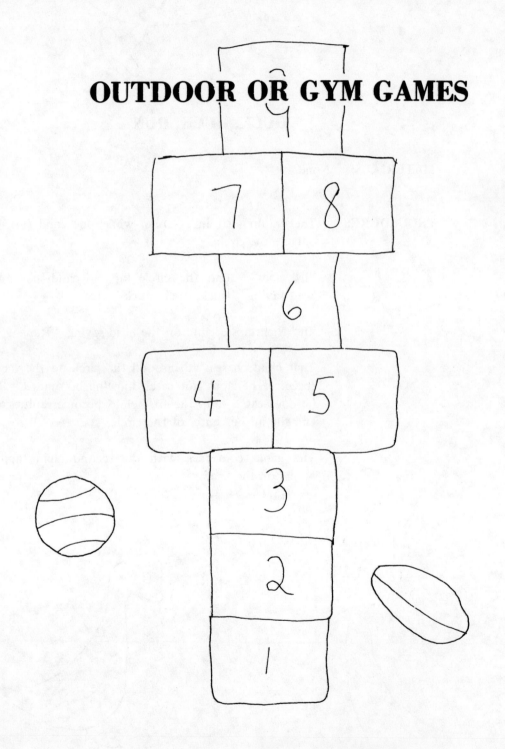

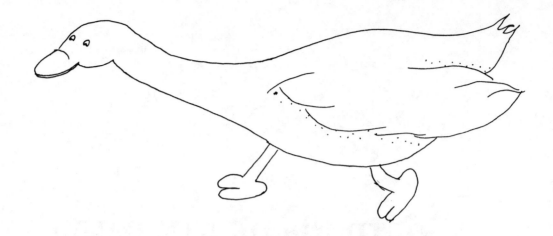

DUCK, DUCK, RUN

MATERIALS: None.

PROCEDURE:
- The children sit in a circle, while one child ("it") is outside the circle.

- "It" goes around the circle tapping children on the head saying, "Duck, duck, duck," etc.

- "It" then taps a child on the head saying, "Run."

- That child chases "it" around the circle to the vacant space. If he does not catch him, he becomes "it." If he does catch him, the first child becomes a duck egg and sits in the center of the circle.

- The game continues with the second child tapping others on the head.

110

SLAP JACK

MATERIALS: None.

PROCEDURE: — The children sit (or stand) in a circle with "it" walking around the outside.

— "It" taps someone on the back and says, "Slap Jack."

— That child then chases him around the circle and tries to catch him before he gets back to the vacant space.

— If he does catch him, that child has to be "it" again. If he does not catch him, the second child becomes "it."

RUN FOR YOUR SUPPER

MATERIALS: None.

PROCEDURE: — Children stand in a circle holding hands.

— One child walks around the outside of the circle and taps the hands of two children. He says, "Run for your supper!"

— The two children run around the circle in opposite directions.

— The first one back is "it." The original "it" steps into the circle where the other two children were.

— Repeat.

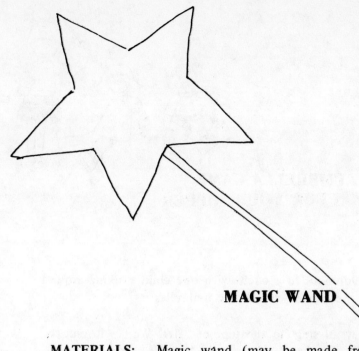

MAGIC WAND

MATERIALS: Magic wand (may be made from dowel rod with a cardboard star covered with aluminum foil taped to the end).

PROCEDURE:

— Choose a child to be the fairy (or witch). Other children spread out around the fairy.

— The fairy waves the magic wand to cast a magic spell, and says, "Abracadabra Zibbity Boo, I now make (lions, snakes, leaves, old men, crying babies, etc.) out of you."

— The children imitate whatever has been named.

— The fairy breaks the spell by saying, "Stop!"

113

UMBRELLA GAME

MATERIALS: Umbrella.

PROCEDURE: — Children sit in a circle with one child walking around on the outside carrying an umbrella.

— They all sing (to the tune of "Here We Go Round the Mulberry Bush"):

What shall we do on a rainy day,
Rainy day, rainy day?
What shall we do on a rainy day,
When we can't go out to play?

— The child with the umbrella selects a child from the circle to go for a walk with him.

— As the two walk around the circle under the umbrella, all sing:

We shall go for a walk today,
A walk today, a walk today.
We shall go for a walk today,
Under the big umbrella.

— These two children join the circle, and another child is selected to carry the umbrella.

— Repeat.

A HUNTING WE WILL GO

MATERIALS: Box large enough for a child to sit inside.

PROCEDURE:
— Children sit in a circle with one child, the fox, walking around the outside. A box is placed in the center of the circle.

— Everyone sings:

  A hunting we will go.
  A hunting we will go.
  We'll catch a fox and put him in a box,
  And then we'll let him go.

— The fox touches a child in the circle on the shoulder.

— That child tries to catch the fox before he can run around the circle and get the space vacated.

— If he is caught, the fox must sit in the box. He stays there until another fox is caught.

— If the fox is not caught, he remains in the space vacated by the other child. Either way, the second child becomes the fox.

— Repeat.

MOUSE TRAP

MATERIALS: None.

PROCEDURE: – Children are divided into two groups, one group becomes the mouse trap, other children are the mice.

– The children form two circles one inside the other – the mouse trap being the inner circle, the mice the outer circle.

– The children on the inner circle join hands and move in one direction, while the children on the outer circle move in the opposite direction.

– When the signal is given (hand clap or drum beat), they all stop moving. Children on the inner circle put up their hands and children on the outer circle move in and out of the trap.

– When another signal is given, the mouse trap closes (the children put their arms down).

– All the mice caught inside have to join the trap.

– The trap is opened (arms raised) and the mice not caught continue to move in and out of the trap.

– Continue until most of the mice have been caught.

CATCH THE SNAKE

MATERIALS: Two or three pieces of rope.

PROCEDURE: — Two or three children are each given pieces of rope.

— The other children try to catch one of the ropes. (They must catch it in their hands, not step on it.)

— When a child catches a rope, he gets to run with it.

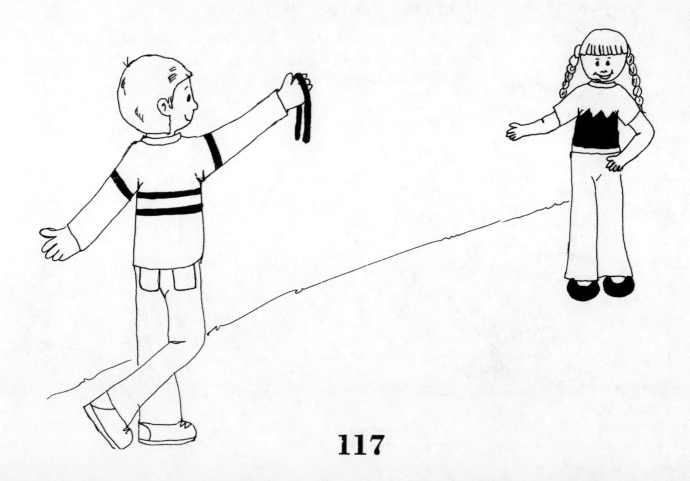

117

FROG IN THE SEA

MATERIALS: Circle.

PROCEDURE: — One child is selected to be the frog and sits in the
                 circle.

               — The other children challenge the frog by running in
                 close to him and saying, "Frog in the sea, can't catch
                 me."

               — When a child is tagged by the frog, he becomes the
                 frog and sits in the circle beside the first frog.

118

BEAN BAG TAG

MATERIALS: Bean bag.

PROCEDURE: — "It" carries a bean bag and all other children chase him.

— If someone tags "it," he gets the bean bag and other children chase him.

— If he wishes to do so, "it" may toss the bean bag away at any time. The child who catches the bag becomes "it" and is chased by other children.

PUSSY IN THE CORNER

MATERIALS: A goal for all but one of the players (i.e., a piece of paper taped down, an "x" on the floor, etc.).

PROCEDURE:
– Goals (called corners) are scattered around the play area. Each child except "it," the Pussy, stands on a corner.

– Pussy walks from one to another and says, "Pussy wants a corner." The other child says, "Go to the next door neighbor." Meanwhile, players try to exchange corners when they have a chance.

– Pussy tries to get corners that other players have left. If Pussy gets a corner, the person left without a corner becomes the new Pussy.

– At any time he chooses, Pussy may call out, "Change corners," and everyone must change.

WIND AND FLOWERS

MATERIALS: Goal line at each end of the play area, line about three feet from one goal line.

PROCEDURE:
— Divide children into two groups. One group is the wind, the other group is flowers.

— Children representing the wind stand on one goal line. Children representing flowers stand on the opposite goal line.

— The flowers choose the name of a kind of flower for their group, then go to the line about three feet from the wind.

— The flowers say, "Wind, who are we?" Wind children guess the names of flowers.

-- When they guess the correct name, the flowers run back to their goal with the wind chasing them.

— Any flowers caught become wind.

— Flowers who were not caught choose a new name and the game continues until all flowers are caught.

BACK TO BACK

MATERIALS: Drum.

PROCEDURE: — The teacher beats out a rhythm on the drum.

— The children move to the rhythm (walk, hop, run, skip, jump, etc.).

— The teacher sounds the predesignated signal (i.e., three rapid beats) and each child must find a partner, stand back to back, lock elbows, and sit down.

— When the drum beat starts again, they must get up (keeping elbows locked if they can) and continue moving to the rhythm of the drum beat.

WILD HORSE ROUND-UP

MATERIALS: A few cowboy hats and/or ropes, an area representing a corral.

PROCEDURE: — A few children are selected to be cowboys, the others are wild horses.

— The foreman of the cowboys yells, "Round 'em up!" and the cowboys catch as many wild horses as they can.

— When a horse is caught, he is put in the corral.

— The last horse caught becomes the foreman and chooses his cowboys.

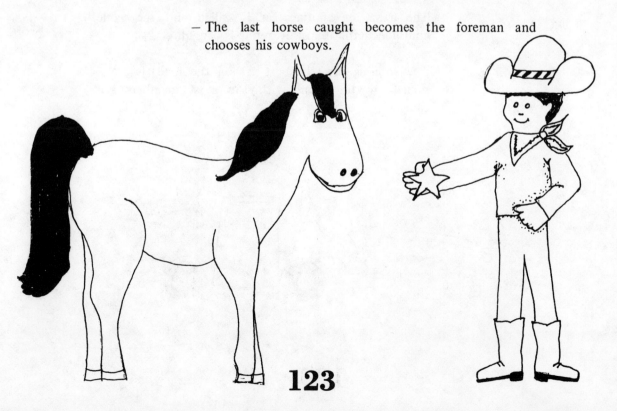

123

CARS

MATERIALS: Four areas representing garages.

PROCEDURE: — One child is chosen to be "it" and the remainder of the children are divided into three groups.

— Each group is given the name of a kind of car and sent to the garage. There will be one empty garage.

— "It" calls out the name of one kind of car.

— The group with that name must run to the empty garage. "It" tries to catch them before they get there.

— Those children caught must stay in the center and help catch others.

— The name of another car is called and the game continues until almost everyone is caught.

— The winning car (the best car on the road) is determined by the team with the most members not caught.

BIRD CATCHER

MATERIALS: Circles marked on the floor or ground.

PROCEDURE: — Divide children into several groups.

— Give each group the name of a bird (robins, sparrows, cardinals, blue jays, eagles, etc.).

— One child is chosen to be the bird catcher.

— The birds are placed in circles representing nests and the bird catcher stands in the center.

— The bird catcher calls out the names of two kinds of birds and those birds must exchange nests.

— The bird catcher tries to catch them as they exchange nests.

— Those who are caught must help the bird catcher when the names of other birds are called.

VARIATION: — This game may also be called dog catcher. Each group is then given the name of a kind of dog and placed in a doghouse.

ONE, TWO, THREE, RUN

MATERIALS: Line at each end of the play area.

PROCEDURE:
— One child is chosen to be "it" and stands in the center of the play area. The other children stand behind a line at one end.

— The child who is "it" says, "One, two, three, run!"

— He then tries to catch them as they run past him to a line at the opposite end of the play area. All children who are caught remain in the center and help catch other children — or a new "it" may be chosen from children not caught.

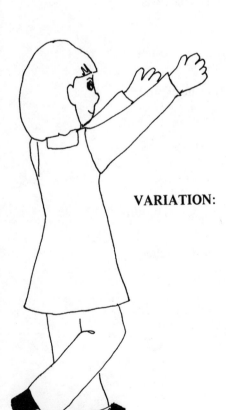

VARIATION:
— Jump, hop, crawl, skip, etc. may be substituted for the word "run."

JET PILOTS

MATERIALS: Goal lines at each end of the play area and you could use the earphones from a listening center and make a microphone by stuffing a child's old sock and inserting a dowel.

PROCEDURE:

— One child is chosen to be in the tower and signal the pilots. He stands to one side wearing the earphones and holding the microphone.

— The other children, the pilots, stand behind a line at one end of the play area.

— When the child in the tower calls, "Tower to pilot, take off!" they race to a line at the other end of the play area.

— When they cross the line they yell, "Checking in!"

— The child who crosses the line first gets to go to the tower and direct the planes.

— Repeat.

SLY OLD PUSSY CAT

MATERIALS: None.

PROCEDURE:
- Divide the children into cats and rats and pair them up so that each cat has a rat.

- The cats follow the rats around saying:

  "Here comes a sly old pussy cat.
  You'd better watch out you bad little rat.
  For pussy has come out to play,
  Now you'd better run away."

- At "run away" each cat chases his rat.

- When each rat is caught, he is taken to the edge of the play area.

- When the rats have all been caught, have the children switch positions and repeat.

CHICKEN AND FOX

MATERIALS: Goal line at each end of the play area.

PROCEDURE:
- Choose one child to be the mother hen and another to be the fox. The other children are chickens.

- The mother hen stands at one end of the play area and the chickens stand at the other end. The fox stands in the middle.

- The mother hen says, "Chickens, chickens, come home to roost."

- The chickens answer, "Mother, we can't. The fox will catch us."

- The mother hen says, "Please come home anyway."

- The chickens run home with the fox chasing them.

- Chickens that are caught become foxes and help catch more chickens when the game is repeated.

HILL DILL

MATERIALS: Goal line at each end of the play area.

PROCEDURE: – One child is selected to be "it" and stands in the center of the play area. The other children stand behind a line at one end.

– The child who is "it" calls "Hill Dill, come over the hill. If you don't run, I'll catch you standing still."

– On the signal, the other children run to a line at the opposite end of the play area while "it" tries to catch as many as he can.

– Those children who are caught must stay in the center and try to catch other children when the game is repeated.

BILLY GOATS GRUFF

MATERIALS: Goal line at each end of the play area.

PROCEDURE:
- Divide the children into two groups. One group will be trolls, the other billy goats.

- The groups stand at opposite ends of the play area.

- The billy goats walk toward the trolls saying, "Trip, trip, trip, etc." until the largest billy goat says, "Tramp, tramp, tramp."

- The goats then turn and run back to their end of the play area with the trolls chasing them.

- All of the goats caught become trolls.

- Repeat.

- When most of the goats have been caught, switch the groups, so that the goats become trolls and vice versa.

COMMENT: This game may be used in conjunction with the story "The Three Billy Goats Gruff."

SQUIRRELS AND TREES

MATERIALS: None.

PROCEDURE: — Divide the children into groups of three with two left over.

— In each group, two children become trees and the other child is a squirrel. The two who are trees join hands in the air and the squirrel stands between them.

— Of the two children not in a group, one is a fox and the other is a squirrel. The fox chases the squirrel.

— When the squirrel thinks he is going to be caught, he can take the place of a squirrel that is in a tree.

— The fox then chases that squirrel.

— If the squirrel is caught, he becomes the fox and the fox becomes a squirrel.

HALLOWEEN

WITCHIE WANTS A SEAT

MATERIALS: None.

PROCEDURE:
— The children sit in a circle with the witch in the center.

— The witch says, "I'm an old witch looking for a seat. When I call your name, I'll see whom I can beat."

— She then calls two names and those children must exchange seats.

— The witch tries to beat one of them to a seat.

— The child left without a seat becomes the witch.

— Repeat.

134

SCAREY THINGS

MATERIALS: None.

PROCEDURE: — Children stand in a circle with "it" in the center.

— Children all walk around the circle saying, "What do we see on Halloween? What do we see on Halloween? We see things that make us scream. That's what we see on Halloween."

— Then they stop walking and "it" points to someone who comes to the center of the circle and imitates a Halloween character.

— The child who guesses who he is imitating becomes "it."

— Repeat.

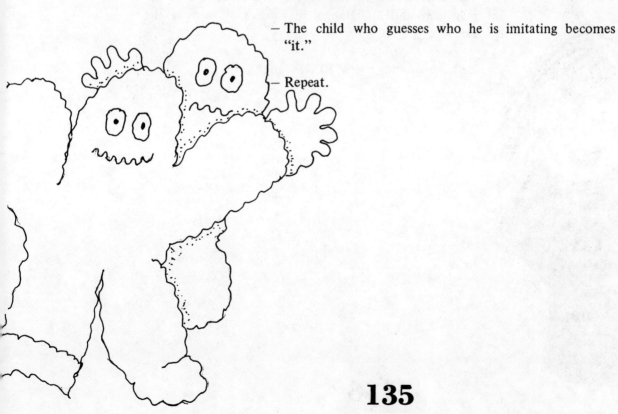

135

OLD MR. HOBGOBLIN

MATERIALS: Goal line at each end of the play area.

PROCEDURE: — One player, Mr. Hobgoblin, stands in the center of the play area. The rest of the children line up on the goal line at one end of the play area. These children are black cats.

— The children say, "Old Mr. Hobgoblin sat on a seat."

— Mr. Hobgoblin answers, "When the cats come running by, I'll chase them down the street."

— The cats all run for the goal at the other end of the play area and Mr. Hobgoblin catches as many as he can.

— He then chooses a new Mr. Hobgoblin.

— Repeat.

136

WITCH'S BREW

MATERIALS: Circle on the floor large enough for all the children to fit inside, a goal at each end of the play area.

PROCEDURE:
- Children walk around inside the circle (witch's pot) with the witch outside the circle stirring.

- The witch says, "The brew is hot." All the children run to the goals at the ends of the play area and the witch catches as many as she/he can.

- The witch chooses a new witch.

- Repeat.

OLD MOTHER WITCH

MATERIALS: None.

PROCEDURE: — Children hold hands and form a circle with one child, the witch, in the center.

— Children in the circle chant:

"Old Mother Witch fell in a ditch,
Picked up a penny and thought she was rich."

— At the word "rich" the children drop hands and run with the witch chasing them.

— The first child caught becomes the witch.

— Repeat.

CHRISTMAS

SANTA'S IN HIS SHOP

MATERIALS: None.

PROCEDURE: — This game is played like Farmer-in-the-Dell.

— The children all walk around in a circle with one child, Santa, in the center.

— Sing the song to the tune of "Farmer-in-the-Dell." On the second verse, "Santa" chooses another child, and that child chooses another on the third verse, etc.

— All children chosen remain the the center of the circle until the last verse. On the last verse, all the children except the "top" return to the circle. The "top" stands in the center alone.

VERSE 1: Santa's in his shop.
Santa's in his shop.
What a scene for Christmas.
Santa's in his shop.

2: Santa takes a drum.

3: The drum takes a doll.

4: The doll takes a train.

5: The train takes a ball.

6: The ball takes a top.

7: They're all in the shop.

8: The top stays in the shop.

AROUND THE TREE

MATERIALS: None.

PROCEDURE: — The words are sung to the tune of "Mulberry Bush."
Act out the words while singing.

VERSE 1: Around the tree the children go,
Children go, children go.
Around the tree the children go,
So early Christmas morning.

2: This is the way we trim the tree.

3: This is the way we bounce our ball.

4: This is the way we walk our dolls.

5: See us run our choo choo trains.

6: This is the way we fly our planes.

7: Jack in the box will jump up high.

8: Repeat the first verse.

141

SANTA CLAUS COOTIE

MATERIALS: Make enough parts for four people to play (and extras in case some get lost.) One die.

Circle for face
Eyes
Nose
Mouth
Beard
Hat

They will last longer if you laminate them or cover them with clear contact paper.

PROCEDURE:

1. The object of the game is to put together Santa's face. Parts are obtained by rolling the die.

2. Each number on the die corresponds to a part of Santa's face.

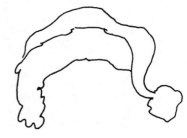

   #1 face
   #2 one eye
   #3 nose
   #4 mouth
   #5 beard
   #6 hat

3. Children take turns rolling the die. They must get a face (#1) before they can get other parts.

4. The first child to complete his face says, "Santa Claus!"

SEE-IF-YOU-CAN
ACTIVITIES

KANGAROO WALK

MATERIALS: Ball for each child.

PROCEDURE: — The child places the ball between his knees and jumps without dropping the ball.

TOP TWISTER

MATERIALS: None.

PROCEDURE: — Jump off the floor and try to turn completely around in the air.

144

AIRPLANE

MATERIALS: None.

PROCEDURE: – The children bend over with one leg out in back and arms out to the sides.

– Children see how long they can stay balanced in this position.

KICKING MULE

MATERIALS: None.

PROCEDURE: – Place hands on the floor and kick feet out behind you.

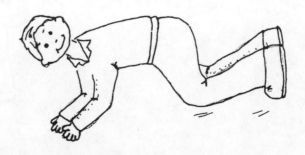

BEAR DANCE

MATERIALS: None.

PROCEDURE: — Bend knees so you're sitting on your heels with arms out in front.

— Kick one foot out in front and bounce back as you alternate feet.

— See who can do this the longest.

TUG OF WAR

MATERIALS: Line.

PROCEDURE: — Divide the children into pairs.

— Each pair of children stands so that the line is between them.

— They hold hands and each tries to pull the other over the line.

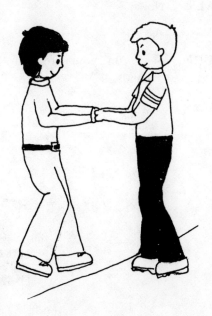

147

THROUGH THE STICK

MATERIALS: Stick (approximately 18 inches long) for each child.

PROCEDURE: – The child holds the stick in both hands, steps over it, passes it over his head, and then repeats.

ROCKER

MATERIALS: None.

PROCEDURE: – Lie on your stomach holding your ankles in your hands.

– Rock.

STRETCH AND TWIRL

MATERIALS: None.

PROCEDURE: — Hold one foot in your hand with leg stretched straight out.

                — Turn around as you hop on the other foot.

TOP

MATERIALS: None.

PROCEDURE: — Put your arms out and close your eyes.

                — Spin like a top.

                — See who can spin the longest without falling down.

COOKING

Cooking!! What a natural way to learn. To take items such as flour, salt and eggs, mix them together . . . smell them, taste them, see them, feel them . . . and come out with a final product of a cake or cookies — what wonderment!!

Encourage the children. Boys and girls can enjoy this as young as three and four years. Begin with easy and fun-to-prepare recipes.

Cooking can be used as a vehicle for learning concepts in many areas. Talk, discuss and interact while you cook — a natural for language development. Learn new words by doing — measuring, mixing, spreading, grating, etc. The observation skills of science can be highly utilized in cooking. Measuring and counting add to math skills. Fine motor co-ordination in stirring, mashing, etc. increase coordination.

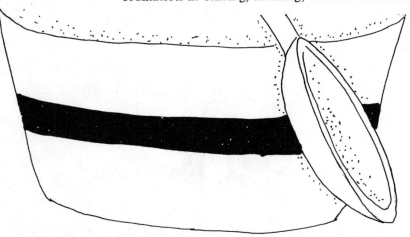

BEFORE THE CHILDREN

START TO COOK

- Wash their hands and clean their fingernails.

- Discuss the recipe — what the final product will be and what ingredients are needed.

- Show them the pans and utensils you will use.

- Take out all the ingredients and measure them.

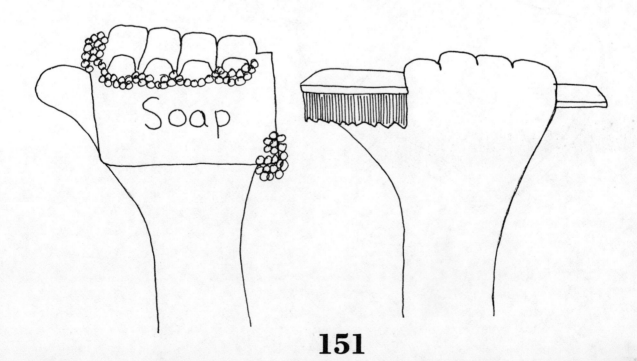

BREADS

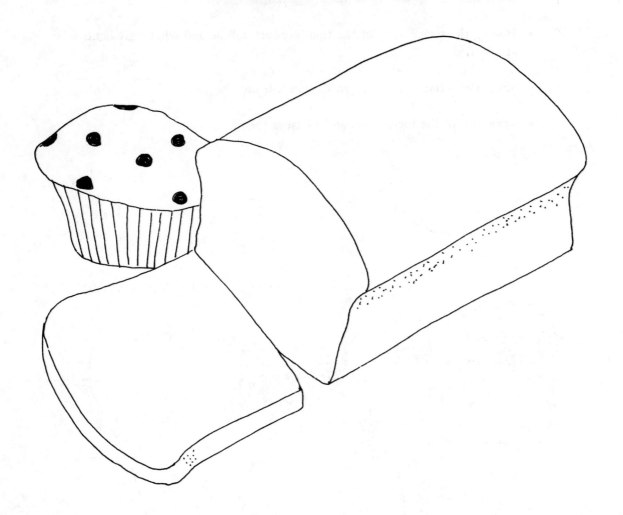

BLUEBERRY MUFFINS

Ingredients:
   box of blueberry muffin mix
   water

Equipment
   bowl
   measuring cup
   mixing spoon
   muffin pan

Directions:
   Follow recipe on blueberry muffin mix (Duncan Hines has real blueberries).

Amount: See directions on the mix.

Comments:
   This activity may be done following the reading of **Blueberries for Sal** by Robert McCloskey.

BLUEBERRY PANCAKES

Ingredients:
2 cups Bisquick baking mix
1 egg
1 cup milk
1/2 cup blueberries
oil (for griddle)
syrup
butter

Equipment
measuring cup
rotary beater
bowl
pancake turner
griddle

Directions:

Beat Bisquick mix, egg and milk with rotary beater in medium bowl until smooth. Fold in blueberries. Pour batter by 1/4 cupfuls onto hot oiled griddle. Turn when bubbles appear. Bake other side until golden brown. Serve with butter and syrup.

Amount: About 18 4-inch pancakes.

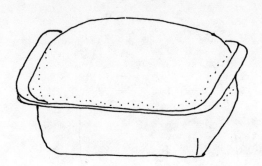

WHITE BREAD

Ingredients:
- 2 pkg. active dry yeast
- 1/2 cup warm water
- 1-3/4 cup lukewarm milk
- 7 cups flour
- 3 T. sugar
- 1 T. salt
- 1 T. soft shortening

Equipment
- bowl
- measuring cup
- tablespoon
- 2 loaf pans — 9" x 5" x 3"
- towel

Directions:

In bowl, dissolve yeast in water. Measure flour. Add milk, half the flour, sugar, salt and shortening to yeast. Beat until smooth and batter "sheets" off spoon. With hand, mix in enough remaining flour until dough cleans the bowl. Turn onto lightly floured board. Cover, let rest 10 to 15 minutes. Knead 10 minutes until smooth and blistered. Place in greased bowl, bring greased side up. Cover with cloth. Let rise in warm place (85 degrees) until double, about one hour. Punch down, cover and let rise again until almost double, about 30 minutes. Divide into two parts. Round up and let rest 10 to 15 minutes. Shape into loaves. Place in greased loaf pans sealed edge down. Grease top of loaf. Cover with cloth; let rise until sides reach top of pan and center is well rounded, 50 to 60 minutes. Heat oven to 425 degrees (hot). Place loaves in center of oven not touching each other. Bake 25 to 30 minutes until golden brown. Test loaf by tapping crust; it should sound hollow.

Amount: 2 loaves

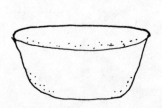

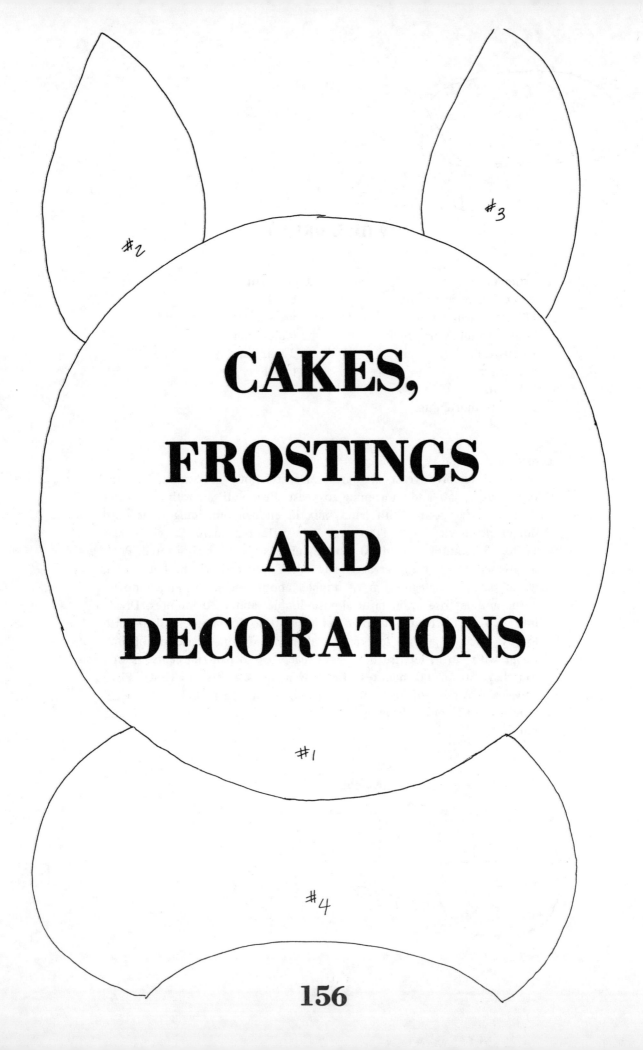

CAKES, FROSTINGS AND DECORATIONS

#2

#3

#1

#4

BUNNY CAKE – DECORATING

Ingredients:
  2 round layer cakes
  1 pkg. coconut
  confectioner's sugar frosting,
    pre-mixed
  jelly beans
  licorice
  food coloring

Equipment:
  cookie sheet
  knife
  spoons
  bowls

Directions:
  Cut, assemble, frost and finish cake as shown.

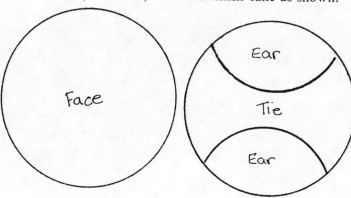

Assemble cooled cake on appropriate surface (i.e. cookie sheet). Frost and decorate with jelly beans and coconut. Decorate bow tie with colored frosting and place jelly beans on it. Use licorice for whiskers. Color some coconut green* and spread around the cookie sheet to resemble grass.

*Mix 2 drops of food coloring with 1 t. water and place in a jar or plastic bag with the coconut and shake.

157

CHOCOLATE CAKE

Ingredients:
  2 cups brown sugar
  2 eggs
  1 cup oil
  1/2 cup cocoa
  1 cup boiling water
  1 cup buttermilk
  1 t. soda
  2-1/4 cups flour
  2 t. vanilla
  grease and flour for pans

Equipment:
  stirring spoon
  bowl
  cake pans
  pot holders

Directions:
Combine all ingredients and bake 25 — 30 minutes at 350 degrees.

Amount: 1 cake

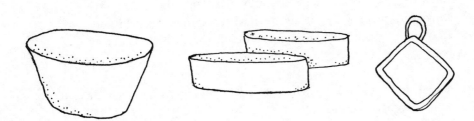

158

CHOCOLATE ICING

Ingredients:
1 cup sugar
2 T. cornstarch
2 T. cocoa
2 T. oleo
1 cup boiling water
1 t. vanilla

Equipment:
bowl
spoon
knife or spatula
measuring spoons
measuring cup
pan

Directions:
Cook until thick. Cool and frost cake.

Amount: To cover one cake.

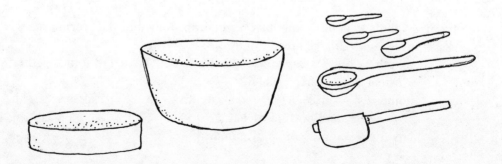

CLOWN CAKE — DECORATING

Ingredients:
   1 9 x 1-1/2" round layer cake
   1 8 x 8 x 2" square layer cake
   1 cup white frosting
   1 cup blue frosting
   1/4 cup red frosting
   gumdrops

Equipment:
   measuring cup
   bowls
   surface on which to
      decorate (hard cardboard)

Directions:
   Cut, assemble, frost and finish cake as shown.

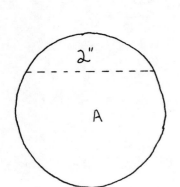
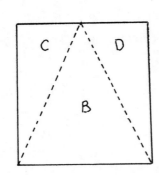
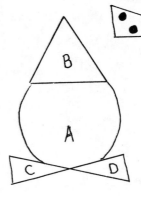

Trim: eyebrows — roll 2 long black gumdrops long and flat. form arches
        eyes — use 2 large green dumdrops.
        mouth — roll 2 large green gumdrops flat. Press and join together;
           cut out to shape smile.
        pompoms — place 3 large red gumdrops in a vertical line at top,
           center, and bottom of hat.
        bow tie — various colors of gumdrops.

HONEY BEAR CAKE — DECORATING

Ingredients:
1 15-1/2 x 10-1/2" layer cake
1 pkg. frosting mix (made up)
decorator's sugar
shoestring licorice
1 black gumdrop
1 marshmallow
1 chocolate chip

Equipment:
knife for cutting and
   spreading

Directions:
Assemble, frost and finish cake as shown.

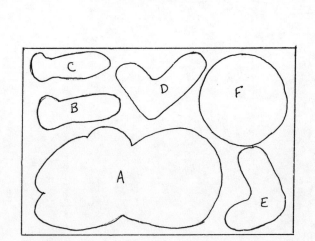

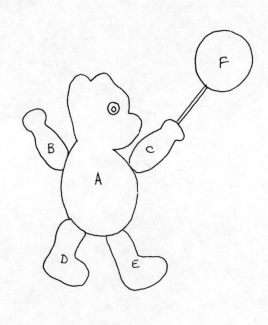

161

COOKIES

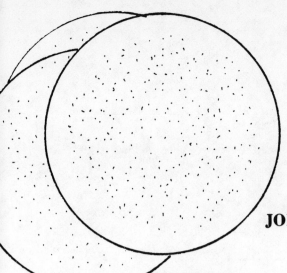

JOHNNY'S SUGAR COOKIES

Ingredients:
1-1/2 cups sifted powdered sugar
1 cup butter
1 egg
1 t. vanilla
1/2 t. almond flavoring
2-1/2 cups flour
1 t. soda
1 t. cream of tartar
sugar (for decoration)
flour (for rolling out)

Equipment:
bowl
measuring cup
teaspoon
sifter
cookie cutters
rolling pin
pastry cloth/old tablecloth

Directions:
Cream sugar and butter. Mix in egg and flavorings. Measure flour. Blend dry ingredients; stir in. Refrigerate 2 to 3 hours. Heat oven to 375 degrees. Divide dough in half and roll out on lightly floured pastry cloth to 3/16" thickness. Cut with cookie cutters. Sprinkle with sugar. Place on lightly greased baking sheet. Bake 7 — 8 minutes.

Amount: 5 dozen cookies.

Comments:
At Christmas time, use Christmas cookie cutters and have the children frost and decorate the cookies.

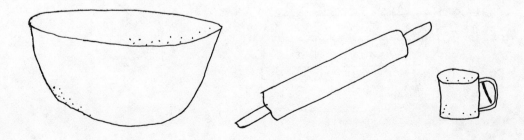

163

NO-COOK COOKIES

Ingredients:
    2 cups white sugar
    1 stick butter
    1/2 cup milk
    2 cups quick oats
    1/2 cup peanut butter
    1 t. vanilla
    7 T. cocoa

Equipment:
    pan
    bowl
    spoon
    waxed paper

Directions:

In pan, mix sugar, butter and milk and boil one minute. In bowl, mix together oats, peanut butter, vanilla and cocoa. Over this, pour the boiling syrup. Mix well and drop by teaspoonful on waxed paper.

Amount: 24 cookies

164

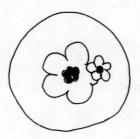

PAINTED COOKIES

Ingredients:
- 3/4 cup shortening (part butter)
- 1 cup sugar
- 2 eggs
- 1 t. vanilla
- 1-1/2 cups flour
- 1 t. baking powder
- 1 t. salt
- 1 egg yolk
- 1/4 t. water

Equipment:
- spoon
- 2 bowls
- measuring cup
- cups
- paint brushes
- rolling pin
- cookie sheet
- cookie cutters

Directions:

Mix well in large bowl shortening, sugar, eggs and vanilla. Blend in flour, baking powder and salt. Cover dough, chill at least 1 hour. Heat oven to 400 degrees. In another small bowl mix egg yolk and water with fork. Divide this mixture among cups to make red, green, blue and yellow paint. Roll chilled dough 1/8 inch thick on lightly floured board. Cut with cookie cutters or make your own interesting shapes. Place on ungreased baking sheet. Using a different paint brush for each color of paint, paint designs on cookies. Bake 6 to 8 minutes until light brown.

Amount: 4 dozen cookies.

PUDDING COOKIES

Ingredients:
   1 pkg. (3 oz.) instant pudding
     (vanilla or coconut cream)
   1 cup Bisquick
   1 egg
   1/4 cup oil
   chocolate chips (optional)

Equipment:
bowl
stirring spoon
measuring cup
cookie sheet

Directions:
Mix well. Drop on cookie sheet. Add chocolate chips for design, if desired. Bake at 375 degrees for 8 minutes.

Amount: 12—18 cookies.

DESSERTS

CHEESE CAKE TARTS

Ingredients:
   2 8 oz. pkg. cream cheese
   1 cup sugar
   1 t. vanilla
   2 eggs
   vanilla wafers
   canned cherries (pie filling)

Equipment:
   cupcake cups
   muffin pan
   spoons
   egg beater
   bowl

Directions:
Whip eggs until creamy (use fork). Mix with cream cheese, sugar and vanilla. Place one wafer in muffin cup. Pour mixture 1/2 full into cups. Bake at 350 degrees for 20–25 minutes. Cool completely. Add cherry topping.

Amount: Serves 18.

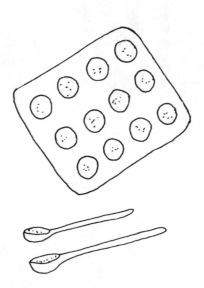

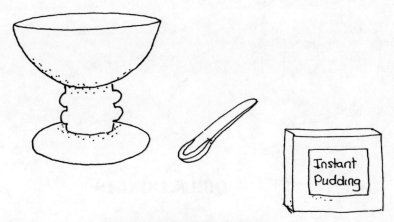

INSTANT PUDDING

Ingredients:
    Instant pudding mix
    milk

Equipment:
    mixer/jar to shake
    measuring cup

Directions:
    Put instant pudding into jar. Add amount of milk indicated on the directions. Shake! Talk with the child and/or children about what is happening.

    Amount: As indicated on pudding box.

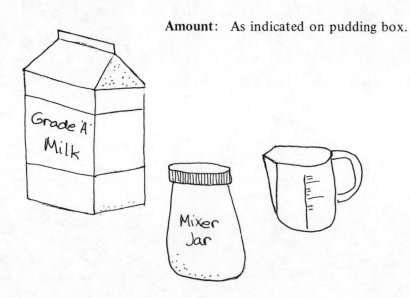

169

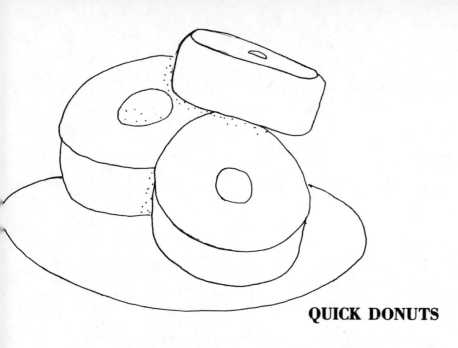

QUICK DONUTS

Ingredients:
    2 or 3 cans of refrigerator biscuits
    oil
    1 box powdered sugar

Equipment:
    frying pan
    doughnut hole cutter or
       small galss
    tongs
    paper towels
    2 paper bags

Directions:

Open cans of biscuits. Punch hole in center of each biscuit with donut hole cutter or small glass. Brown holes and donuts in 1/2 inch oil, on each side. Use tongs to pick them up. Drain on paper towel. Pour 1/2 box powdered sugar into doubled paper bags. Place 2 − 3 donuts in bag and shake to coat; repeat the process.

Amount: 16 − 24 donuts and holes.

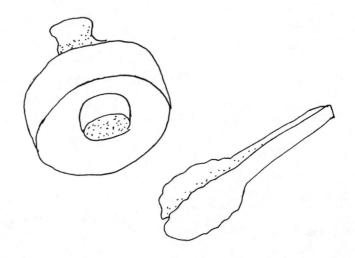

DRINKS

ORANGE JUICE

Ingredients:
oranges

Equipment:
knife
orange squeezer
pitcher

Directions:
Pass the oranges around. Look at their skins. Are they thick? Thin? What is their shape, color, texture? Which orange is heavy? Light? Cut the orange in half. Observe seeds and segments. Turn the orange halves in the squeezer. Pour into pitcher. Drink. Compare with canned orange juice.

Amount: 4 oranges provide 2 small glasses of juice.

GRAPE FROST

Ingredients:
    1 6 oz. can frozen grape
      (lemon) punch concentrate
    5 to 6 cups finely crushed ice

Equipment:
    1 can opener
    blender
    cup or glasses
    1 measuring cup

Directions:

Empty punch into chilled bowl of electric blender. Add ice, 1 cup at a time. Blend well after each addition. Serve at once.

Amount: 7 to 8 cups.

BROWN COW

Ingredients:
    1 scoop chocolate ice cream
    1 glass root beer

Equipment:
    spoon
    glass

Directions:
    Place 1 scoop ice cream into a glass of root beer.

Amount: Serves one.

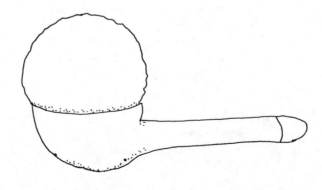

174

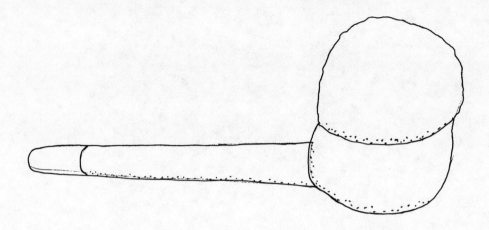

PURPLE COW

Ingredients:
    1 scoop vanilla ice cream
    1 glass grape soda

Equipment:
    spoon
    glass

Directions:
    Place 1 scoop vanilla ice cream in tall glass of grape soda.

Amount: 1 serving.

175

MAIN DISHES

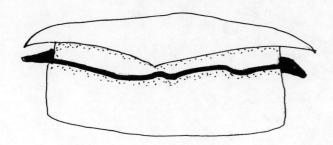

CHEESE DREAMS

Ingredients:
   6 English muffins
   12 slices bacon
   3 tomatoes, sliced
   12 slices cheese

Equipment:
   1 baking sheet
   1 pancake turner
   pot holders

Directions:

Split muffins and toast them and bacon under the broiler. Toast muffins on one side. Broil bacon until crisp. Top each muffin with tomato slice, bacon slice (cut in half) and slice of cheese. Broil until cheese melts.

Amount: 12 servings.

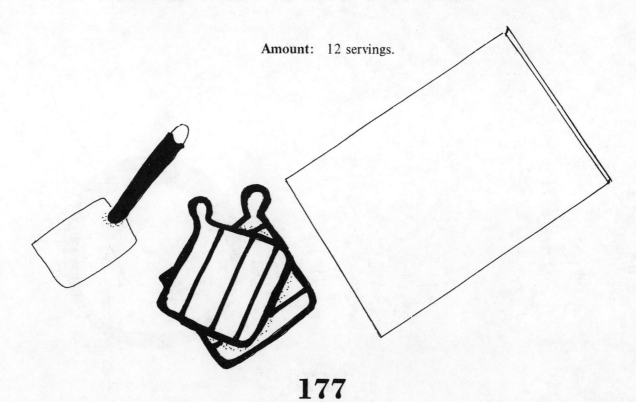

177

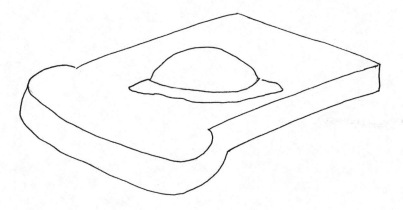

EGGS IN A NEST

Directions:
Take slice of bread and cut out center of bread slice (use glass upside down). Spread both sides of bread with soft butter. Brown bread slice in skillet over medium-high heat. Turn bread over. Break into a cup 1 egg and carefully slip the egg into the hole in the bread slice. Lower heat; cover skillet and cook until egg white is set. Sprinkle egg with salt. Remove from pan with pancake turner.

Amount: Increase the recipe by any number needed.

178

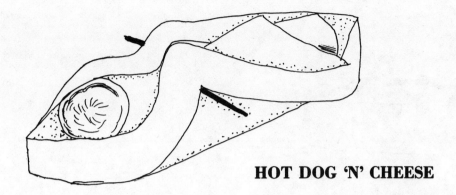

HOT DOG 'N' CHEESE

Ingredients:
8 hot dogs
8 slices bread
soft butter
prepared mustard
8 slices American cheese
1/4 cup butter

Equipment:
sauce pan
knife (table)
cookie sheet
tooth picks

Directions:
Drop into a sauce pan of boiling water the 8 hot dogs. Lower heat, cover and simmer 5 to 8 minutes. Spread 1 side each of the 8 slices of bread with soft butter and mustard. Place bread slices on baking sheet and top each with a slice of American cheese. Place a hot dog on top of each cheese slice. Fold over to make a triangle shape. Fasten with tooth picks. Melt in small pan 1/4 cup butter and brush each triangle with melted butter. Broil 4 to 5 inches from heat about 2 minutes.

Amount: 8 servings.

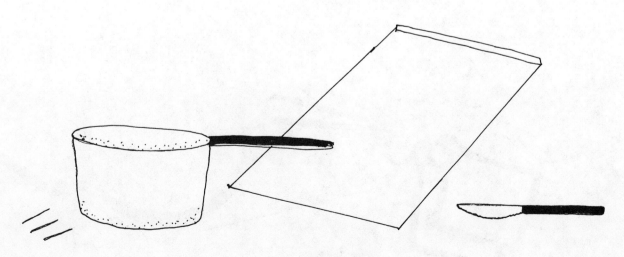

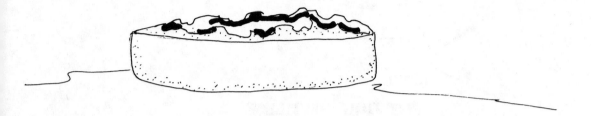

PIZZA BURGERS

Ingredients:
  6 English muffins
  1 can pizza sauce
  6 — 8 ozs. pizza cheese

Equipment:
  table knife
  can opener
  baking sheet
  pancake turner
  pot holders

Directions:
  Split muffins in half. Spread pizza sauce on each half. Sprinkle cheese on top — enough to suit your taste. Bake in oven until cheese melts. (Toaster oven for 5 minutes at low temperature).

  Amount: 12 small pizza burgers.

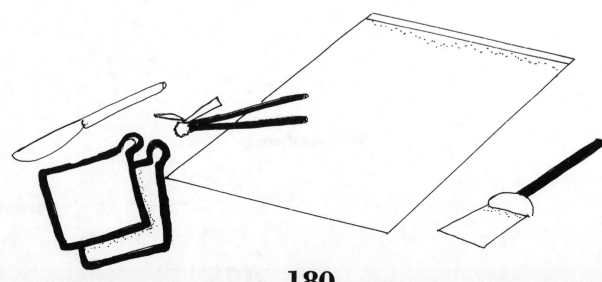

180

SCRAMBLED EGGS

Ingredients:
    eggs (as desired)
    salt
    touch of milk
    butter

Equipment:
    bowl
    egg beater
    frying pan

Directions:

Each child cracks his/her own egg and places it in a bowl. Each child whips his egg, adds a little milk and salt. Melt a little butter in the frying pan and pour in egg mixture.

Amount: Adjust the number of eggs to desired quantity.

SLOPPY JOES

Ingredients:

   2 T. margarine
   2 T. onion flakes
   1 green pepper (chopped)
   1 lb. ground beef
   1 8 oz. can tomato paste
   1 t. salt
   1 t. pepper

Equipment:

   pan
   large apron
   teaspoon
   paring knife

Directions:

Melt margarine in pan. Brown onion, pepper and ground beef. Add tomato paste, salt and pepper. Stir until well mixed. Serve on buns.

Amount: 5 – 6 servings.

NIBBLES

BANANA POPS

Ingredients:
2 T. butter
3 T. water
1 pkg. chocolate fudge frosting
4 bananas
nuts

Equipment:
double boiler
skewers

Directions:
Melt butter, add frosting mix (dry) and stir until smooth. Heat over boiling water for 5 minutes, stirring often. Peel bananas, cut crosswise into 3 or 4 pieces and place each on a wooden skewer. Dip into fudge mixture. Roll in chopped nuts. Chill until fudge coating is firm.

Amount: 12 – 16 pops.

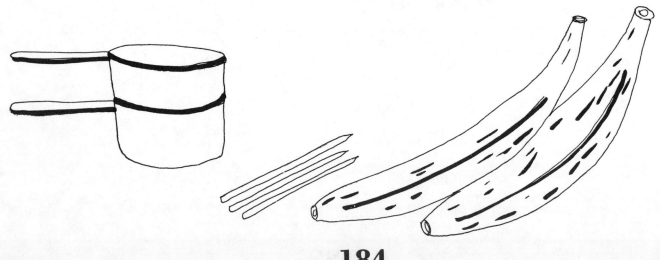

CARAMEL APPLES

Ingredients:
  8 medium apples
  2 T. butter
  3 T. water
  1 pkg. caramel frosting
  chopped nuts (optional)

Equipment:
  skewers
  pan
  spatula

Directions:
Wash and dry apples, insert skewers in them. Melt butter, add frosting mix (dry) and stir. Heat 5 minutes and stir often. Remove from heat. Dip apples one at a time in caramel mixture. Dip in chopped nuts, if desired. Add a few drops of hot water if caramel mixture becomes too thick. Do last apples with a spatula.

Amount: 8 apples.

CHEERIOS — FUDGE

Ingredients:
1 pkg. chocolate fudge frosting mix
1/2 cup soft margarine
2 t. hot water
1/2 t. vanilla
2 cups Cheerios

Equipment:
bowl
fork

Directions:
In bowl, combine frosting mix (dry), butter, water and vanilla with fork or fingers until thoroughly blended. Add Cheerios; mix well. With hands shape into one inch balls. Roll in 1/2 cup crushed Cheerios.

Option:
1/2 cup peanut butter may be added to this.

Amount: 4 dozen.

CHOCOLATE ANGELS

Ingredients:
    1 angel food cake (2 loaf pans)
    milk chocolate candy bars
    marshmallows

Equipment:
    knife
    baking sheet

Directions:
    Cut cakes into 1 inch slices. Top each slice with chocolate candy bar squares (use 1 oz. candy bars). Place marshmallow halves on chocolate squares. Place angels on baking sheet about 4 inches from broiler, 1 to 2 minutes, or just until marshmallows brown. Serve immediately.

Amount: 18 Angels.

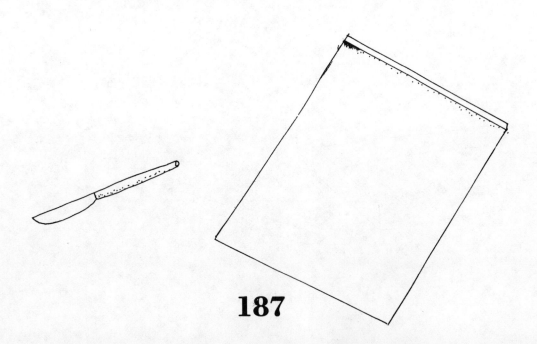

187

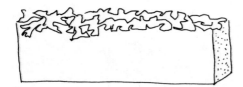

COCONUT BARS

Ingredients:
   layer cake
   2 cups coconut
   powdered sugar

Equipment:
   measuring cup
   knife
   cake in pan, 15-1/2 x 10-1/2 x 1"

Directions:
Prepare any layer cake mix and pour into greased pan. Sprinkle 2 cups coconut over top of batter. Bake 25 – 30 minutes. Cool. Sprinkle powdered sugar over top while warm. Cut into bars to serve.

Amount: 18 – 24 bars.

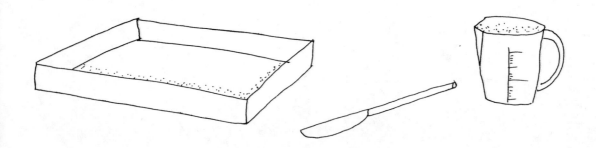

FROZEN CHEERIOS SQUARES

Ingredients:
- 1 pkg. chocolate malt frosting mix
- 1/4 cup butter or margarine
- 3 T. hot water
- 1/2 t. vanilla
- 3 cups Cheerios
- 1/2 cup peanuts

Equipment:
- bowl
- spoon
- square pan, 9 x 9 x 2"

Directions:

In large bowl, combine dry frosting mix, butter, water and vanilla until blended. Stir in Cheerios and peanuts. Spread in a lightly buttered pan. Freeze for 2 to 3 hours. Cut into 1-1/2" squares; serve frozen.

Amount: 3 dozen.

GUM BALL CHRISTMAS TREE

Ingredients:
  2 bags jelly bean candy

Equipment:
  1 box tooth picks
  styrofoam cone
  1 round base (optional)
  drop of any color (optional)

Directions:
  Place tooth picks on cone. Put candy on picks. Trim base with ribbon or felt.

Amount: 1 tree.

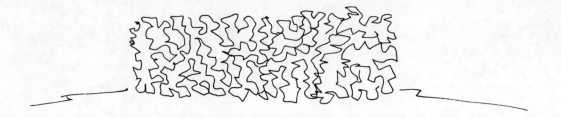

HONEY COCONUT BARS

Ingredients:
  leftover cake
  soft butter
  honey
  flaked coconut

Equipment:
  baking sheet

Directions:
  Heat oven to 350 degrees. Slice leftover cake into 3 x 1-1/2" strips.
  Coat each strip with soft butter and honey. Roll in flaked coconut.
  Place strips on baking sheet. Bake 10 — 12 minutes. Serve warm.

Amount: As desired.

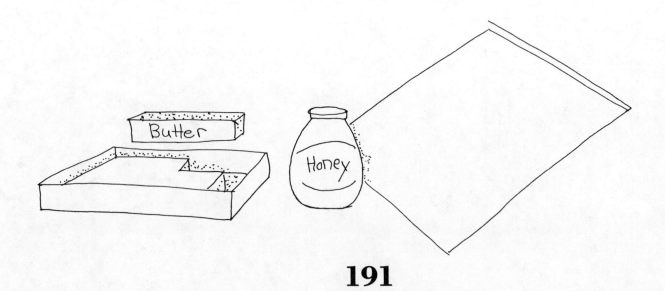

JELLY-COCONUT DIPS

Ingredients:
    any flavor layer cake mix
    jelly
    coconut
    nuts (optional)

Equipment:
    pan, 15-1/2 x 10-1/2 x 1"

Directions:
Heat oven to 350 degrees. Prepare any layer cake mix as indicated on package. Pour batter into greased pan. Bake 25 to 30 minutes. Cool in pan. Cut into 1-1/2 inch squares. Dip sides and tops into jelly softened by heating over hot water. Roll in coconut, or roll in nuts (finely chopped).

Amount: 70 dips.

NIBBLES

Ingredients:
   5 cups Golden Graham cereal
   1 cup dry roasted peanuts
   1/4 cup butter
   1/4 cup peanut butter
   1 T. cinnamon
   1 cup raisins*

Equipment:
   bowl
   stirring spoon
   tablespoon
   measuring cup
   13" x 9" baking pan

Directions:
Mix the cereal and peanuts together and then spread in the baking pan. Melt together the butter, peanut butter and cinnamon. Pour this mixture over cereal and nuts. Mix until well coated.

*Place raisins in the pan as an option. Bake at 350 degrees for ten minutes. Cool.

     Amount: Serves 15 children as "nibbles."

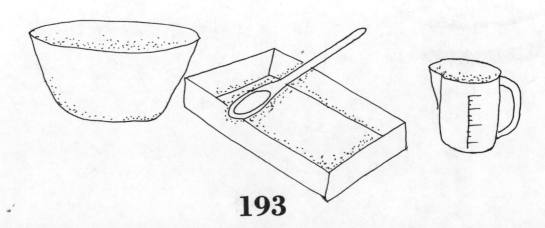

PEANUT BUTTER BALLS

Ingredients:
    marshmallow fluff
    peanut butter
    vanilla wafers

Equipment:
    bowl
    spoon
    measuring cup
    rolling pin
    waxed paper

Directions:

Place vanilla wafers between two sheets of waxed paper and crush with a rolling pin. In bowl mix equal parts marshmallow fluff and peanut butter. Blend. Form into balls. Roll into crushed vanilla wafers.

Amount: Adjust the amount of ingredients to desired quantity.

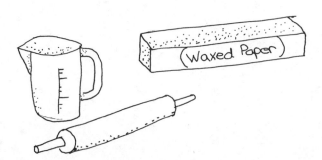

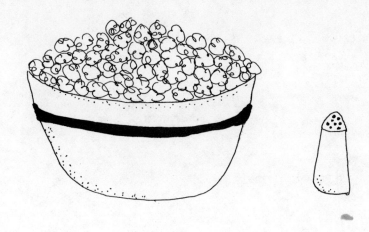

POPCORN

Ingredients:
popcorn
oil
salt

Equipment:
popcorn popper or pan
bowls

Directions:
Place a little oil in the bottom of pan. Heat. Add popcorn kernels and pop. Add salt.

Amount: As desired.

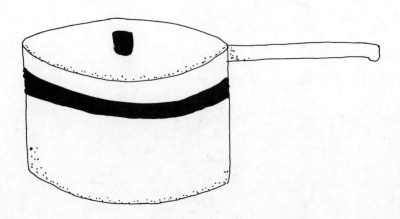

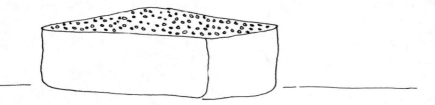

TOASTED CAKE

Ingredients:
   leftover cake
   butter
   cinnamon—sugar

Equipment:
   knife
   broiler pan

Directions:

Cut leftover cake into wedges. Split and spread with soft butter. Sprinkle with a cinnamon—sugar mixture. Toast under broiler 1 – 2 minutes about 3 inches from heat.

Amount: As desired.

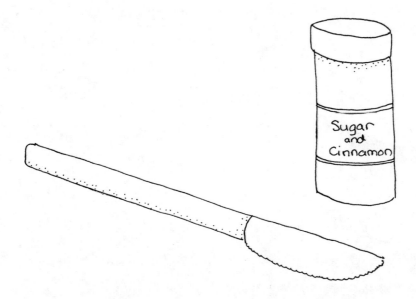

SNO CAPS

Ingredients:
  1 pkg. small marshmallows
  2 small pkgs. semi-sweet
    chocolate bits
  1/4 cup oleo
  1 cup peanut butter

Equipment:
  foil
  9" square pan
  sauce pan
  stirring spoon
  table knife

Directions:

Line a 9" x 9" pan with foil. Cover the bottom with marshmallows. Melt oleo and chocolate bits. Add peanut butter — mix well. Pour mixture over marshmallows and chill. Turn out onto a piece of foil and cut into squares. Makes a checkerboard design.

Amount: 16 — 20 squares.

197

WHITE CLOUDS

Ingredients:
  white frosting mix
  chopped nuts
  40 soda crackers

Equipment:
  baking pan
  knife
  bowl for frosting

Directions:

Heat oven to 350 degrees. Prepare white frosting mix as directed. Fold in 1 cup chopped nuts. Drop by teaspoonful onto 40 soda crackers. Bake 4 — 6 minutes or until light brown.

Amount: 40.

SANDWICH
FILLINGS

BUTTER

Ingredients:
   whipping cream
   salt
   yellow food coloring

Equipment:
   baby food jars
   waxed paper

Directions:

Pour a small amount of whipping cream into 4 oz. sterilized baby food jar. Place a piece of waxed paper over the opening before putting on lid. (Each child may have individual churn.) Shake . . . shake . . . shake! It takes a while. Music with a "beat" would be an appropriate background. A lump will form in the bottom, leaving buttermilk and butter. Pour off buttermilk; add salt to taste. Discuss color of butter. Add coloring.

Amount: A little to taste.

200

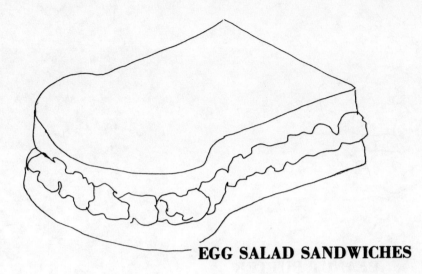

EGG SALAD SANDWICHES

Ingredients:
  1 hard boiled egg per child
  salt
  mayonnaise
  2 slices bread per child

Equipment:
  small bowls
  forks
  table knives
  tablespoon

Directions:
Children peel and wash their own eggs. Place in small bowl and mash. Add 1 tablespoon mayonnaise and a pinch of salt. Spread on bread and eat!

Amount: Adjust ingredients to desired quantity.

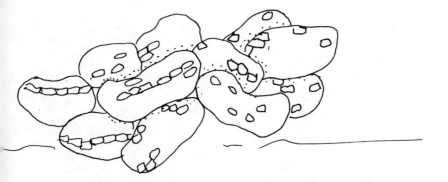

PEANUT BUTTER

Ingredients:
  1 lb. roasted peanuts
  few drops peanut oil
  little salt

Equipment:
  blender

Directions:

Shell 1 pound roasted peanuts. Place peanuts in blender and grind up.
Add a few drops of peanut oil for moisture and add a little salt.
Refrigerate.

Amount: 1 cup peanut butter.

SOUPS

CHICKEN SOUP WITH RICE

Ingredients:
   1 large can Bounty chicken broth
   1 large can water
   4 chicken bouillon cubes
   1 small onion (chopped)
   several carrots and celery (chopped)
   1-1/2 cups rice
   salt and pepper to taste

Equipment:
   hot plate
   large pot
   spoon
   styrofoam cups
   spoons

Directions:
Mix all ingredients in pot and simmer slowly until vegetables are tender.
Serve in styrofoam cups.

Amount: 12 – 15 servings.

STONE SOUP

Ingredients:

		Equipment:
1 stone	parsnips	pot
5 beef bouillon cubes	tomatoes	spoon
1 qt. water	celery	knife
1 can tomato or V-8 juice	cauliflower	
carrots	beans	
potatoes	corn	
turnips	peas	
onions	small bag of noodles	

Directions:

Scrub the stone well. Dissolve 5 beef bouillon cubes in 1 quart water. Add tomato or V-8 juice and simmer, add more water when necessary. Wash and chop all vegetables and cook in pot 30 minutes. Add a small bag of noodles during last ten minutes.

Amount: 2 quarts soup.

Comment:

This activity may follow the reading of the **Stone Soup Book**.

VEGETABLE-BURGER SOUP

Ingredients:
  1/2 lb. ground beef
  1 1 lb. can (2 cups) stewed
    tomatoes
  1 8 oz. can (1 cup) tomato sauce
  2 cups water
  1 10 oz. pkg. frozen mixed
    vegetables
  1/2 envelope (1/4 cup) dry
    onion soup mix
  1 T. sugar

Equipment:
  pot
  spoon
  measuring cup
  bowls

Directions:
  Brown ground beef, Pour off excess fat. Add remaining ingredients.
  Bring to a boil, reduce heat, cover and simmer 20 minutes.

Amount: 6 — 8 servings.

VEGETABLES AND FRUITS

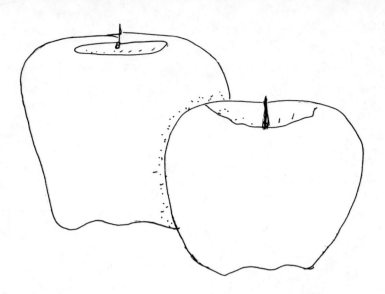

APPLE SAUCE

Ingredients:
    several apples
    sugar
    water
    cinnamon

Equipment:
    hot plate
    pan, bowl, spoon
    table knives
    food mill

Directions:

Wash apples. Have children cut apples into small chunks. Place in pan with a small amount of water. Cook until soft. Add sugar and cinnamon to taste. Strain through food mill.

If you do not have access to a food mill or strainer, be sure to peel and core apples before cooking.

Amount: 4 apples make approximately 2 servings.

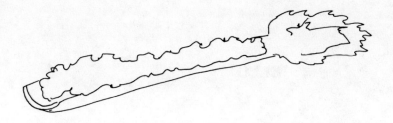

CELERY CANOES

Ingredients:
  celery
  cream cheese, cheese whiz
    or peanut butter

Equipment:
  table knives

Directions:
    Clean celery. Cut into 3" lengths. Using knife fill with cream cheese, cheese whiz or peanut butter.

      Amount: As desired.

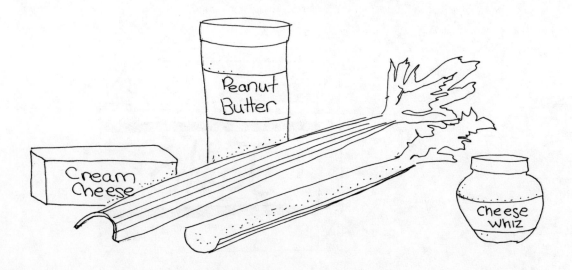

JELLO

Ingredients:
    1 large package Jello — any color
    1 pkg. miniature marshmallows
    water

Equipment:
styrofoam cups
pan
bowl
spoon

Directions:
    Pour Jello into bowl. Add 2 cups boiling water and 2 cups cold water. Pour Jello into individual styrofoam cups. Let each child add marshmallows to his own Jello (a good counting experience).

Amount: Serves 15 — 20.

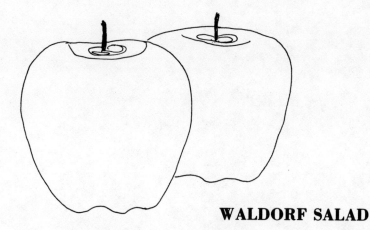

WALDORF SALAD

Ingredients:
 2 apples
 3 celery stalks
 1/2 t. lemon juice
 1/4 cup mayonnaise
 1/2 cup chopped nuts
 lettuce

Equipment:
 paring knife
 bowl
 measuring cup
 spoon

Directions:
Wash apples and cut into quarters. Cut celery and apples in small pieces. Sprinkle with lemon juice. Add nuts and mayonnaise. Mix. Serve on lettuce leaf.

Amount: Serves 2 – 3.

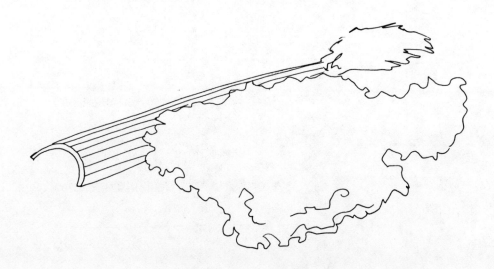

SCIENCE

Discovery and exploration is the basis for a child's learning and playing. Adults working with children extend the curiosity of the child by providing an environment that lends itself to observation and exploration.

A variety of experiences will produce discovery and learning. The following "hands-on" activities will help increase awareness by means of observation, discussion, and experimentation of "doing."

ACTIVITY: **AIR**

OBJECTIVE: To observe that air is real and occupies space.

MATERIALS: Two glasses, large basin and water.

PROCEDURE: Place one glass under the water and let it fill. Push the other glass, open end down, straight down into the water and it will be full of air. Move the glass full of water over the glass full of air so that when you tip the glass of air, the bubbles will pour upward into the glass of water, pushing the water out. You can pour the air back and forth from glass to glass in this matter.

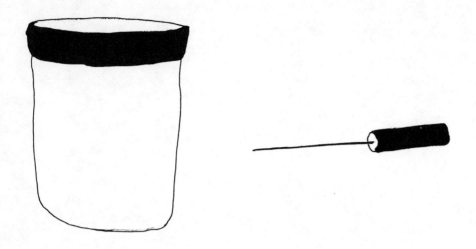

ACTIVITY: **AIR PRESSURE**

OBJECTIVE: To observe that air presses.

MATERIALS: Glass jar with lid, water.

PROCEDURE: Fill a glass jar with water. Punch two holes in the lid and screw it on tightly. Invert. Notice how water comes from one hole. Put your finger over one hole. What happens?

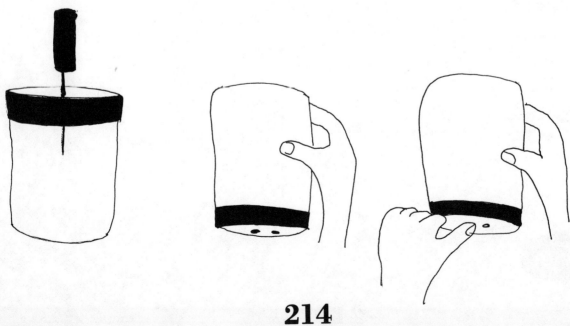

ACTIVITY: **SINKING AND FLOATING**

OBJECTIVE: To observe objects that float or sink and why?

MATERIALS: Large container of water, and stone, cork, styrofoam, nails, screws, feather, spools, cups, wood, etc. Baby food jar.

PROCEDURE: Into a large container of water (aquarium), drop a stone and a cork to observe why one floats and one does not. Try a variety of other objects to observe floating differences.

VARIATION: Place in the water one small (baby food) jar without a lid. Try same jar with a lid. Put a little sand in jar. Cap. Keep adding more and more sand in jar until it sinks. Do the same with water. What happens? Why? Air helps things float — balloons, wood, cork, our lungs, etc.

215

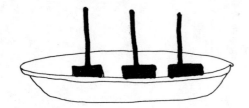

ACTIVITY: **CHEMICAL INDOOR GARDEN**

OBJECTIVE: To introduce a simple chemical reaction to the children.

OBJECTIVE: Shallow dish (pie plate), 2 or 3 lumps of soft coal or coke, salt, bluing, and ammonia, glue, twigs.

PROCEDURE: Place coal in the shallow dish with a little water. Glue twigs or sticks on top of coal for trees. (Let glue dry before completing the garden.)

Mix 6 tablespoons salt with 6 tablespoons bluing and 6 tablespoons of ammonia. Pour this mixture slowly over the coal.

To give the garden some color, use food coloring, colored inks, or fabric dye in a medium dropper, drop the different colors all over the mixture. In a short time crystals will form. Drop on more ammonia if needed.

216

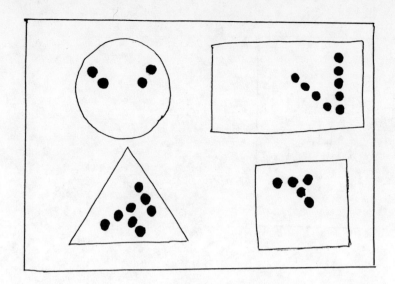

ACTIVITY: **COLOR DESIGN**

OBJECTIVE: To classify according to color.

MATERIALS: Felt tip pens and stryofoam.

PROCEDURE: Using a felt tip pen, draw separate areas (circles, squares) of different colors on a piece of styrofoam. Give the child golf tees or push pins to stick into the styrofoam, matching the color of the tee or pin to the color of the area drawn.

VARIATION: Have child create own designs on the styrofoam with different colored markers. Then match the area drawn.

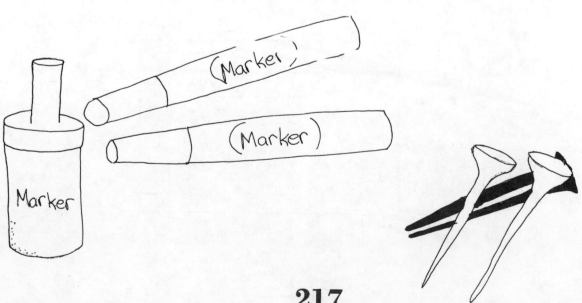

ACTIVITY: **GOING SHOPPING**

OBJECTIVE: To increase the child's memory and classification con-
              cepts.

MATERIALS: Pictures of grocery items pasted on cards.

PROCEDURE: Begin with three pictures on a card, increasing the
              number gradually for greater difficulty of task. The child
              is permitted to study the card for a short period of time,
              then goes shopping without the card to get all articles on
              the "list."

VARIATION: The same procedure can be done with household pictures
              and then shopping within the house.

Toothpaste

ACTIVITY: **SHAPE SEARCH & SHAPE COLLAGE**

OBJECTIVE: Classification according to shape.

MATERIALS: Scissors, magazines and paste.

PROCEDURE: Suggest that the child look through a magazine for objects that are a certain shape. Cut out the shapes and make a collage of the shapes.

ACTIVITY: **PASTING WITH COLORS**

OBJECTIVE: Classification according to color.

MATERIALS: Scissors, magazines, and paste.

PROCEDURE: The child first searches through magazines for pictures of a certain color, or looks through a box of fabric scraps or pieces of gift wrap, etc. The child then pastes them on a piece of paper.

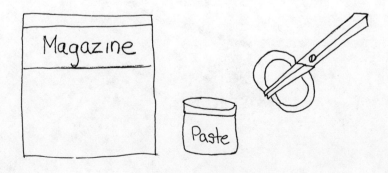

219

ACTIVITY: **CONSERVATION**

OBJECTIVE: To observe that rain has a great impact on the soil.

MATERIALS: Saucer with soil, white paper, and medicine dropper with water.

PROCEDURE: Place a saucer with soil on a piece of white paper. Fill a medicine dropper with water and hold it above the soil. Release water a drop at a time and observe how much soil is splashed out on the paper. Place a clean sheet of paper under the saucer. Again release drops but hold an obstacle such as a pencil in the path of the drop to break the force of the rain drop. Do plants prevent the wearing away of the soil in this way?

ACTIVITY: **LIGHT**

OBJECTIVE: To observe that light travels from one place to another in a straight line.

MATERIALS: Mirror and sunshine.

PROCEDURE: Stand in a window and use a mirror. Hold the mirror in such a way that the bright sunlight hits it. Move it slowly about. You will find a reflection on the wall. As you move the mirror, the sunlight on the wall moves. The rays come from the sun — hit the mirror — and are bounced or reflected to the wall. The light travels in a straight line to the mirror and then to the wall where you see it.

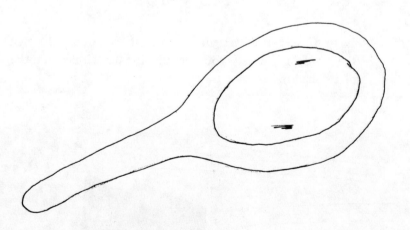

ACTIVITY: **LIGHT**

OBJECTIVE: To observe that light travels from one place to another (in a straight line).

MATERIALS: Piece of glass 6" square, black paper 6" square and wax paper the same size, lamp.

PROCEDURE: Light a lamp and hold the glass between you and the lamp. Now hold the wax paper up between you and the lamp. Try the black paper in the same way. You discovered that light went through the glass and you could see through it. Light went through the wax paper, but you could not see through it. Light did not go through the black paper and you could not see through it. Glass is transparent, wax paper is translucent and black paper is opaque.

VARIATION: Now cut a circle in the black paper and hold it to the lamp and notice the shadow it makes. The shadow is round like the circle and square like the paper.

CONCEPT: Light travels in a straight line and it cannot go through the black paper, so you see the lighted circle and the black shadow.

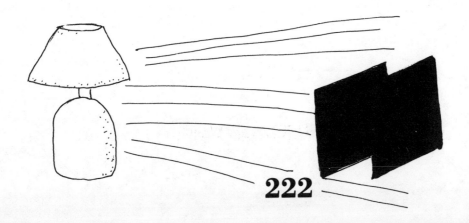

222

ACTIVITY: **TERRARIUM**

OBJECTIVE: To observe living creatures and build an environment similar to their own.

MATERIALS: Terrarium, soil, water, twigs, food, small creatures such as snakes, turtles, salamanders, and cameleons.

PROCEDURE: Set up the container.

ACTIVITY   **ANT HILL**

OBJECTIVE: To observe ants reconstruct their home.

MATERIALS: Ants and ant hill, 2 pieces of glass and wood.

PROCEDURE: Bring in an ant hill with the ants. Place them between two pieces of glass. Cover the other surfaces with wood. Watch the ants reconstruct their home. Make available to them both crumbs and water.

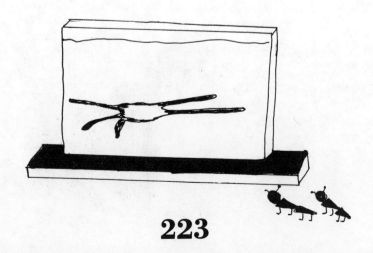

223

ACTIVITY: **COLLECTING INSECTS**

OBJECTIVE: To observe and learn about insects.

MATERIALS: Net and baby food jars.

PROCEDURE: Have the children catch a variety of small insects. Display them in baby food jars (with holes in cap) as a small zoo. Discuss living habits of the insects.

VARIATION: Place insects in a cup (grasshoppers, ants, etc.) and watch them via a magnifying glass covering the top.

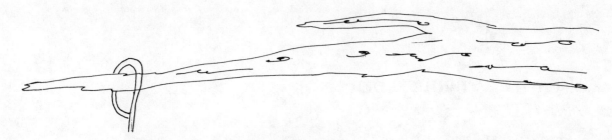

ACTIVITY: **BIRD FEEDER**

OBJECTIVE: To feed birds and observe a variety of birds while they feed.

MATERIALS: Paper cups, bird seed, melted suet or lard, string.

PROCEDURE: Fill paper cups (almost full) with bird seed. Pour in just enough melted suet or lard to stick seed together. Stir. Place a string in the center for hanging. Place cup in freezer until very hard. Tear off paper cup and hang in a tree.

ACTIVITY: **BIRD FEEDER**

OBJECTIVE: To feed birds and observe a variety of birds while they feed.

MATERIALS: Cheerios, heavy string, large needle, cranberries, and popcorn.

PROCEDURE: String Cheerios on heavy string and hang on a tree. A large needle can be threaded and the children can string cranberries and popcorn.

ACTIVITY: **HANGING PEANUT BUTTER BIRD FEEDER**

OBJECTIVE: To feed birds and observe a variety of birds while they feed.

MATERIALS: String, strips of suet, peanut butter, bird seed.

PROCEDURE: Tie pieces of string to strips of suet. Smear suet strips with peanut butter and then roll in bird seed. Hang in trees.

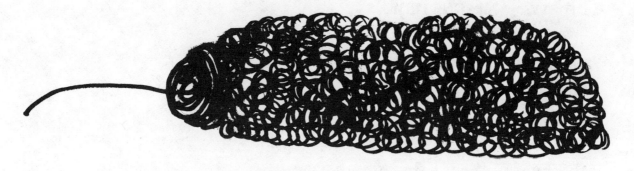

ACTIVITY: **COCOONS**

OBJECTIVE: To observe the life process and change of a particular living creature.

MATERIALS: Large container and water.

PROCEDURE: Find a cocoon (often found on trees after the leaves have fallen). Place in a large container or cage and sprinkle occasionally with water.

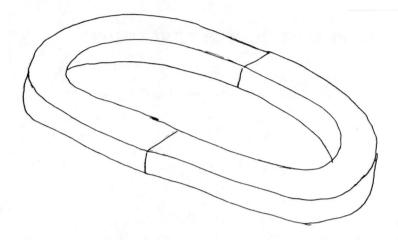

ACTIVITY: **MAGNETISM**

OBJECTIVE: To have the child play with magnets and learn their laws.

MATERIALS: Magnets.

PROCEDURE: Have each child play with magnets and verbalize what is happening. If we bring the north end of another magnet up to the north end of a suspended magnet, it will repel it. If we bring the south end of the magnet up to the north end of a suspended magnet, it will attract it.

1) Unlike magnetic poles attract.

2) Like magnetic poles repel.

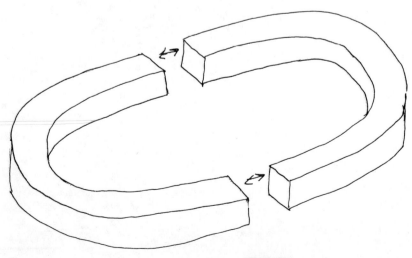

228

ACTIVITY: **PAPER CUP PLANTING**

OBJECTIVE: To observe various plants grow.

MATERIALS: Desired seeds, soil, and paper cups.

PROCEDURE: Have the children plant seeds in soil in little paper cups. Keep on a window sill for light. Water frequently. Various seeds could be orange, grapefruit, lemon, grass, beans, flower.

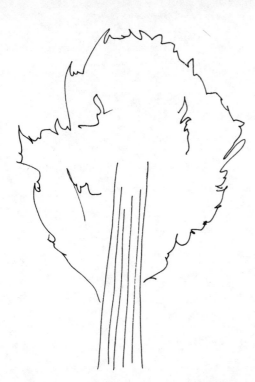

ACTIVITY: **CELERY MAGIC**

OBJECTIVE: To experiment and observe capillary action.

MATERIALS: Celery, colored water, glass.

PROCEDURE: Place stalks of celery into glasses of colored water. Watch what happens. Compare to pictures of the human body and its veins.

ACTIVITY: **SPROUTING SEEDS**

OBJECTIVE: To observe sprouting seeds.

MATERIALS: Lima beans, cotton, 2 pieces of glass, container, water.

PROCEDURE: Place several lima beans on a layer of cotton between two layers of glass. Tape the panes together and stand on edge with the bottom edge in water. Leaves, roots, and stems will develop if kept wet.

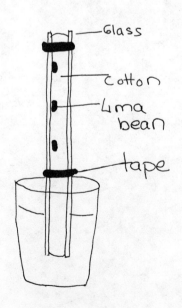

ACTIVITY: **SAND**

OBJECTIVE: To experiment and observe with self-exploration.

MATERIALS: Sand and some container (table or box).

PROCEDURE: Have children experiment in such areas as roads, ditches, and tunnels with trucks, shovels, buckets, sifters, spoons, and numerous containers that stimulate the imagination of young children.

VARIATION: The addition of water changes the consistency and makes it easier to shape and manipulate.

SUGGESTIONS: Set limits (no throwing). Spread canvas, plastic or newspapers on floor.

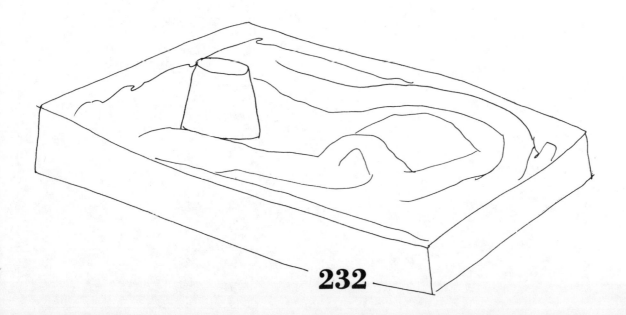

232

ACTIVITY   **SMELL**

OBJECTIVE: To increase experimentation and knowledge of smells.

PROCEDURE: 1) Make a variety of smell bottles for the children to experience and identify. Suggested items include:

garlic	almond	vanilla
cedar	banana	cucumber
camphor	soap	wet wool
lemon	cloves	orange
onion	lime	cologne
coffee	strawberry	vinegar
flowers	peppermint	

2) Make a smell board: Drop cotton balls into various liquid solutions. Glue them on a piece of cardboard. Let the child sniff and tell what is on each cotton ball.

3) At suppertime, can the child guess what's for dinner without peeking or going into the kitchen.

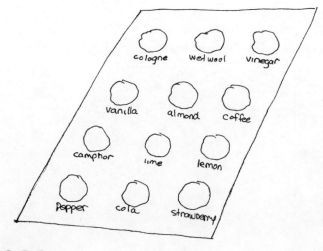

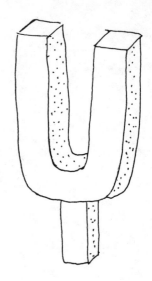

ACTIVITY: **SOUND**

OBJECTIVE: To increase the awareness of sound.

PROCEDURE: 1) Sit very still and have the children just listen. Help them identify what they hear. Labeling sounds enables children to increase their vocabulary and to increase their awareness to the many things that do create sound.

2) Teach children to rap a tuning fork on the table to make a vibration. Then listen.

3) Rap a tuning fork and dip it into a glass of water. Watch it make waves.

4) Have the children make paired sound cans (set of 6) and compare to find like and different sounds. Fillings might include:

corn	noodles
rice	pins
marbles	corn meal
beans	salt
liquid	nuts

234

ACTIVITY: **SOUND**

OBJECTIVE: To observe that sound travels in waves.

MATERIALS: None.

PROCEDURE: Have a child stand near the door, but where he cannot be seen. Listen while he sings a note or two. Why can you hear him when you cannot see him? Because sound can travel around corners. Light cannot. Sound waves usually move out in all directions from the object that is vibrating.

ACTIVITY: **SOUND**

OBJECTIVE: To observe that sounds are made by rapid vibration of things.

MATERIALS: Empty bottle, grass, etc.

PROCEDURE: Blow an air stream across the mouth of an empty bottle. Try different size bottles. Place a blade of grass between thumbs and blow.

ACTIVITY: **TASTE**

OBJECTIVE: To increase experimentation and knowledge of taste.

PROCEDURE: 1) Cook as much as possible. Explore the raw form and the transformation as they cook.

2) Try blindfolded taste tests, allowing the children to dip their fingertip and then taste a variety of solids and liquids: salt, sugar, catsup, syrup, pudding, honey, vinegar, spices, etc.

3) Compare tastes and textures of raw versus cooked using the same foods in the two different states. For example, apples, broccoli, cauliflower, mushrooms, cranberries, pears, etc.

4) Let the child taste opposites, compare them — salty, sweet, bitter, sour, etc.

ACTIVITY: **HOT AND COLD**

OBJECTIVE: To measure temperatures of hot and cold.

MATERIALS: Two glasses, hot and cold water, thermometer.

PROCEDURE: Fill glass with hot water and another with cold water. Feel each with your finger. Compare and discuss. Now measure the temperatures with a thermometer. Put some water from each glass into a third one. Feel and measure temperature.

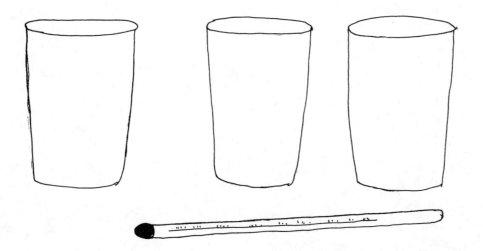

ACTIVITY: **MELTING**

OBJECTIVE: To observe the process of melting.

MATERIALS: Sugar, sand, salt, glasses of water.

PROCEDURE: Sprinkle sugar, sand and salt into separate glasses of water to observe melting.

VARIATIONS: 1) Bring in snow allowing children to see it melt into water and dirt.

                    2) Catch snowflakes in your hand. Use a magnifying glass to see the snowflakes and watch them melt and turn to water in your warm hands.

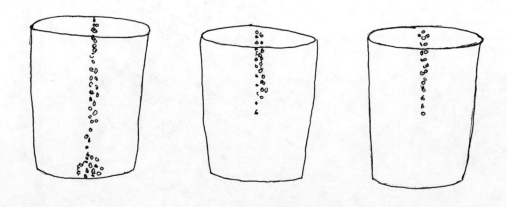

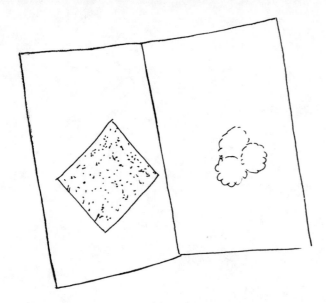

ACTIVITY: **TOUCH ME BOOK**

OBJECTIVE: To broaden the awareness of the touch sense (also will broaden the child's vocabulary).

MATERIALS: Paper for pages, appropriate "touch" surfaces.

PROCEDURE: Talk about different textures such as smooth, soft, bumpy, scratchy, hard, spongy, sticky, etc.

Have the child find examples of these and paste them on pages in his book. Examples could be saran wrap, cotton, corrugated paper, sand paper, popsicle stick, sponge, and scotch tape.

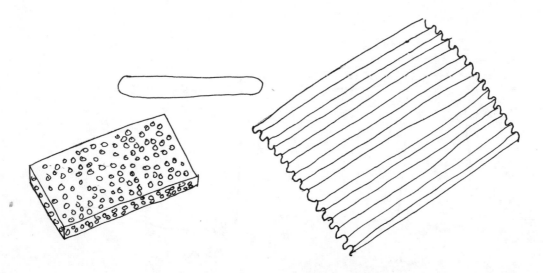

ACTIVITY: **FEEL BOX**

OBJECTIVE: To increase the experimentation of "touch."

MATERIALS: Box and all kinds of objects.

PROCEDURE: Make a feel box in which the children can reach to identify a familiar object which they cannot see. Some objects might include:

button	shoelace	barrette
comb	washcloth	soap
toothbrush	screw	pliers
pencil	scissors	Q-tip
band aid	sponge	sock
fork	spoon	cup

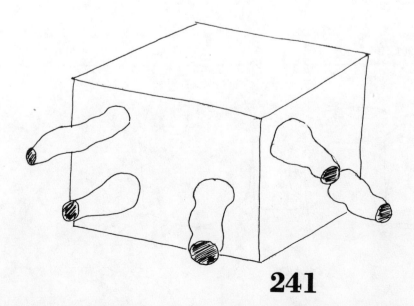

241

ACTIVITY: **WATER**

OBJECTIVE: To experiment and observe with self-exploration (pouring and measuring).

MATERIALS: Water, container, utensils of measurement.

PROCEDURE: The water is available in some container (sink, water table, pool or large dish pan). Have available unbreakable utensils such as measuring cups, funnels, strainers, squirt bottles, egg beaters, straws, clothes sprinklers, wire whips, medicine droppers, etc.

1) A child can learn about sizes, shapes, and measurement by playing with an array of containers from which to pour. Have him compare water going from large containers into smaller one and vice versa: from short, fat containers into tall, narrow ones.

2) Add food coloring to water for added dimensions. You can also bring in color concepts.

ACTIVITY: **EVAPORATION**

OBJECTIVE: To view the process of evaporation.

PROCEDURE: 1) Have the children wet a handkerchief and place over a radiator or heat duct to observe evaporation.

2) Place the same amount of water into identical clear plastic glasses. Mark water level on exterior with marking pen or rubber band. Cover one. Observe change level from day to day.

3) Into two flat dishes put a mixture of salt and water, and a water only. After evaporation, discuss residue and/or lack of residue. Taste it.

4) Paint the sidewalk with water. What happens?

5) Wipe a chalkboard with a wet sponge and blow or fan it. What happens?

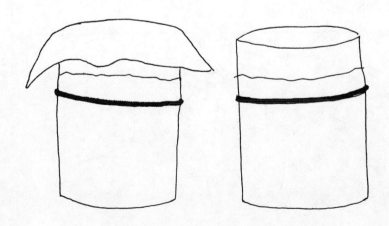

243

ACTIVITY: **FREEZING**

OBJECTIVE: To observe the process of freezing.

MATERIALS: Containers (all shapes), water.

PROCEDURE: Freeze water in a cone-shaped paper cup, a balloon, milk carton, etc. Remove containers and discuss shapes and that water will take the shape of any container into which it is put.

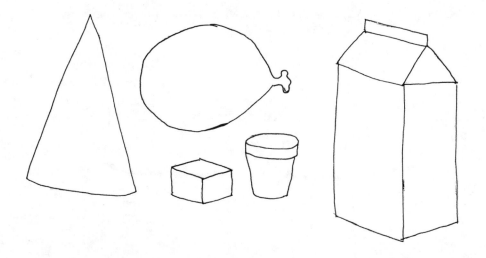

ACTIVITY: **WEATHER CLOCK**

OBJECTIVE: To become aware and observe types of weather.

MATERIALS: Paper plates, crayons, arrow, fastener.

PROCEDURE: Make a paper plate weather clock with the sun, snow
                (cotton), gray cloud, umbrella and rain, and a wind-
                blown kite. Attach a large arrow in the center and use to
                point out the weather daily. Children love taking turns
                being the "weather person."

ACTIVITY: **WEIGHT BOXES**

OBJECTIVE: To classify likenesses and differences with weight.

MATERIALS: Opaque tins or boxes, salt, sand, pebbles, etc.

PROCEDURE: Fill cans with materials, make two of each: 2 empty ones, 2 one-quarter full, 2 half full, and 2 completely full. Scramble the boxes or cans on the floor, and let the child try to unscramble them by finding the boxes or cans that are the same weight.

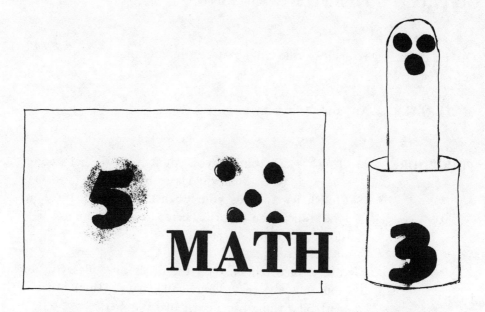

MATH

Many learning experiences combine scientific and mathematical concepts. It is important that children be exposed to concrete experiences and this contribution to their growing perceptual development will add a good solid base for later cognitive learning.

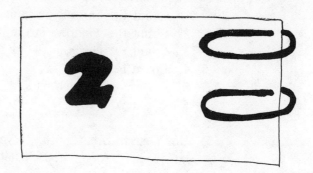

ACTIVITY: **TIPS FOR COUNTING**

OBJECTIVE: To increase the child's success in counting.

MATERIALS: Any objects nearby.

PROCEDURE: 1) Touch every thing as you count it. Say, "Let's count the spoons to find out how many there are. One (touch it), two (as you touch the second), three (as you touch the third). There are four spoons. Why don't you count them?"

2) Every so often, mix up the order of things you are counting so that your child won't think that a particular thing has a particular number.

3) Have all the things you are going to count in front of you, in other words, don't start by trying to count the houses you pass while riding in a car.

4) Count different things:
   1. Count the buttons on your coat.
   2. Count the windows in the living room.
   3. Count the chairs in the kitchen.
   4. Count pennies.
   5. Count your french fries.
   6. Count your toys.

5) Don't rush. Don't push. If your child doesn't seem interested — forget it. He'll let you know when he's ready to learn.

ACTIVITY: **NUMBER ORDER**

OBJECTIVE: To provide practice in counting.

MATERIALS: Ten 4" x 3" cards, pen.

PROCEDURE: Draw one circle on the first card, two on the second, three on the third and so on, until all the cards have circles on them. Place the cards on the table or on the floor. Be sure that they are not in order. Ask, "Can you put them in order?"

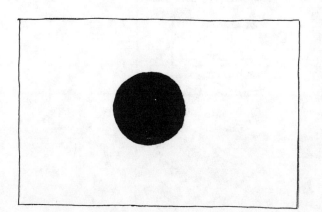 

ACTIVITY: **COUNT OUT**

OBJECTIVE: To provide practice in counting and the meaning of numbers.

MATERIALS: Piece of cardboard and counters (buttons, stones, candy, bottle caps or macaroni).

PROCEDURE: At the top of a piece of posterboard or paper, print the numerals 1 — 5 for younger children or 6 — 10 for older children. The child then places the correct number of counters below the printed numerals.

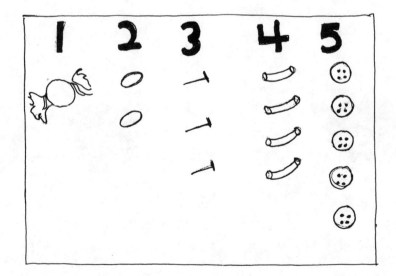

ACTIVITY: **CORN IN A CARTON**

OBJECTIVE: To provide practice in counting, number recognition and one to one correspondence.

MATERIALS: Egg carton, popcorn (or other small materials), and pen.

PROCEDURE: On the side of each cup within the egg carton, print a number from 1 – 10, scramble their position. The child then places the correct number of counters with each numeral.

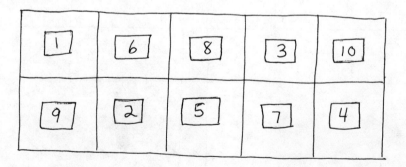

251

ACTIVITY: **PUZZLE NUMBER CARDS**

OBJECTIVE: To provide practice in the meaning of numbers.

MATERIALS: Posterboard, scissors, and pen.

PROCEDURE: Divide a half a piece of posterboard 6 inches by 3 inches. Down the middle draw a zig zag line. Cut along this line. On one half print a number. On the other half print the numeral dot array ., .., ..., etc. Repeat the process for all numbers for 1 — 9. The child then tries to match each array and numeral. If the halves make a whole, the child is correct.

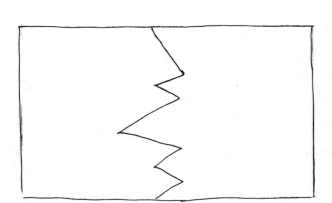
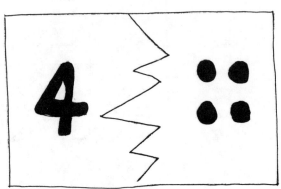

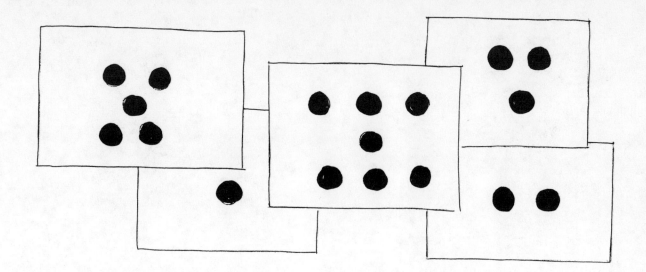

ACTIVITY: **SHOPPING GAME**

OBJECTIVE: To increase counting and numeral recognition concept.

MATERIALS: Objects of child's choice, flash cards with dots representing 1 — 10.

PROCEDURE: Give child the flash cards. Have him "shop" around the room buying as many articles for which his number calls. Child may use grocery bag or market basket.

VARIATION: Use regular flash cards (1 — 10) when child recognizes them.

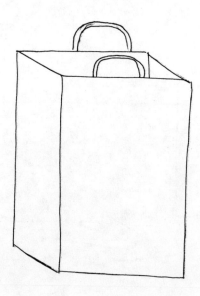

ACTIVITY: **PINCUSHIONS**

OBJECTIVE: To increase counting and numeral recognition concept.

MATERIALS: Make a set of number cards (1 — 10) with a pincushion on each one (foam rubber works well), pins.

PROCEDURE: Have the child stick the appropriate pins in each pincushion. Then order them from one through ten.

ACTIVITY: **CLIP A NUMBER**

OBJECTIVE: To provide practice in counting, number recognition and one to one correspondence.

MATERIALS: Cards and paper clips.

PROCEDURE: Use cards with a numeral (1 – 10) and a corresponding number of dots. The child then places paper clips on the edge of the card to correspond to the numeral. The cards can then be placed in order from one through ten.

255

ACTIVITY: **NUMBER CANS**

OBJECTIVE: To increase the child's success in counting.

MATERIALS: Orange juice cans or milk cartons painted with spray paint, tongue depressors.

PROCEDURE: Place dots on the containers representing numerals 1 — 10. The child places the correct number of tongue depressors into each container.

VARIATION: Place simple addition problems on containers and have children answer by placing the appropriate number of depressors in the container. Example: 1 + 1, 2 + 1, 4 + 2, . . .

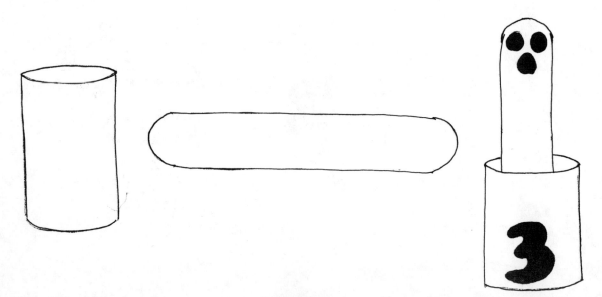

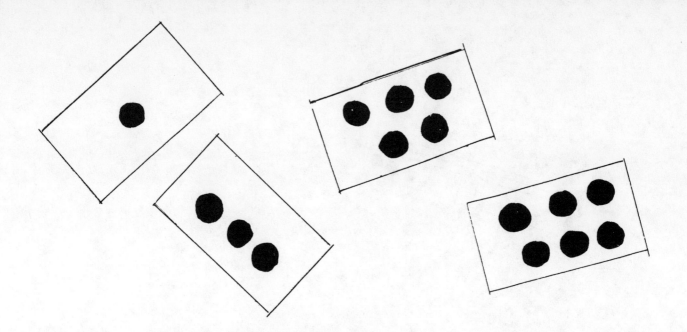

ACTIVITY: **MISSING NUMBERS**

OBJECTIVE: To provide practice in counting.

MATERIALS: Ten 4" x 3" cards, pen.

PROCEDURE: Draw one circle on the first card, two on the second, three on the third and so on, until all the cards have circles on them. Place the set of cards on the table or on the floor. Ask your child to close his eyes while you hide one of the cards. When he opens his eyes, ask, "Can you figure out which card I have?"

257

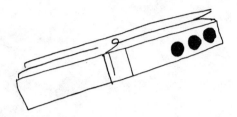

ACTIVITY: **PIN ON**

OBJECTIVE: To provide practice in recognizing numerals.

MATERIALS: Cheese box and clothes pins.

PROCEDURE: On the side of an empty cheese box, print either numerals 1 — 9 or dot arrays ., .., ..., etc. On the clothes pins print either dot arrays or numerals. The child then tries to match the clothes pins with the correct numerals or array on the cheese box. He does this by clipping the clothes pins on the box.

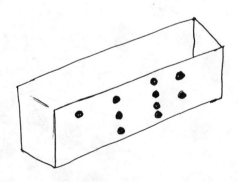

ACTIVITY:	**BUTTON TOSS**

OBJECTIVE:	To provide practice in counting.

MATERIALS:	Shopping bag, buttons (5 to 20), yardstick or adhesive tape.

PROCEDURE:	Fold down the top of a paper bag and place it on the floor. (A book in the bottom of the bag will keep it from toppling over.) Make a line on the floor, a reasonable distance from the bag. You'll have to experiment to find the right distance. Say, "Stand behind this line. Throw one button at a time. See how many you can get in the bag." When all the buttons have been thrown, count the number of buttons in the bag. That's your score. Then gather up all the buttons and try again.

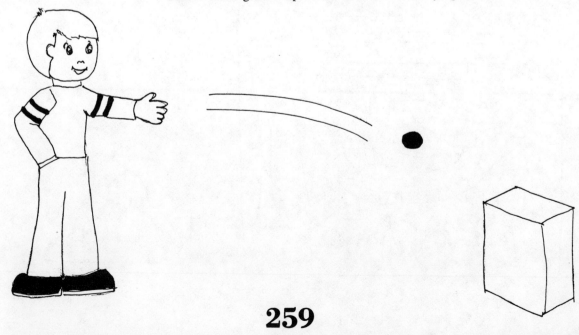

ACTIVITY: **RACE TO UNCLE SAM'S HOUSE**

OBJECTIVE: To provide practice in recognizing numerals and their number value.

MATERIALS: A playing board with a route from home to Uncle Sam's shown in a chain of 40 squares. Tiny cars (paper will do) of different colors, one for each player. A set of 50 cards on each of which is a numeral from 0 to 9.

PROCEDURE: Shuffle cards and place them face down. Each player selects a car. In turn, each child draws a card and moves his car as many squares as the numeral indicates. The first one who gets to Uncle Sam's house wins.

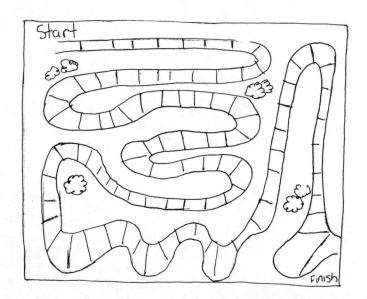

ACTIVITY: **GOING HUNTING**

OBJECTIVE: To increase counting and numeral recognition concept.

MATERIALS: Objects of your choice.

PROCEDURE: Ask the child to find one (your choice) item and bring it to you. The "big hunter" returns with his "catch" for the day. Continue, in like manner, with the other numerals up to 10.

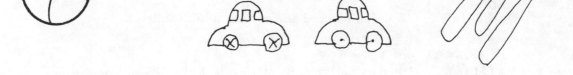

ACTIVITY: **COUNTING CARDS**

OBJECTIVE: To increase counting and numeral recognition concept.

MATERIALS: Dot or flash cards (0 – 10).

PROCEDURE: See if the child can name all the numerals on the flash cards. Bounce a ball the number of times shown on the card. Or, clap hands the number of times stated on each card. Let the child choose the method to demonstrate.

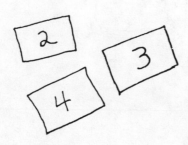

ACTIVITY: **GARAGES AND CARS**

OBJECTIVE: To match numeral representation of quantity.

MATERIALS: Put dots on the roofs of 10 cars. Make garages from half gallon milk cartons. Put a numeral (1 – 10) on the roof of each garage.

PROCEDURE: The child proceeds to park the car in the corresponding garage.

ACTIVITY: **POCKETS**

OBJECTIVE: To help the child match the correct numerals with sets.

MATERIALS: Shirt cardboard, pictures of different sets (1 — 10),
              pockets or envelopes, cards with 1 — 10 on them.

PROCEDURE: Place the 1 — 10 sets on shirt cardboard with a pocket
              under each set. The child will place the correct numeral
              card in the pocket.

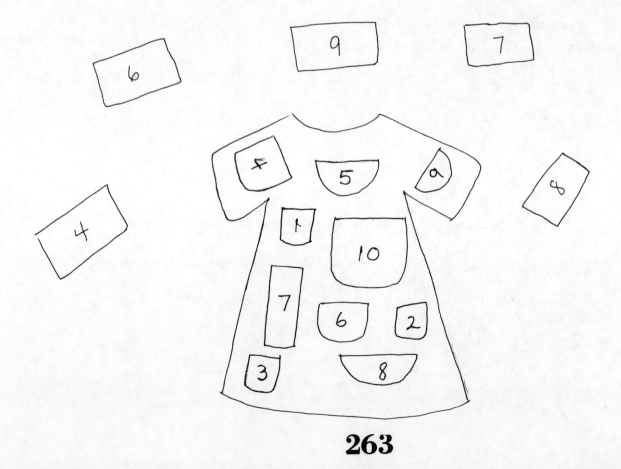

ACTIVITY: **FLOWERS AND VASES**

OBJECTIVE: To provide practice in counting and number recognition.

MATERIALS: Small plastic containers, large vase, plastic flowers, pin.

PROCEDURE: Each small plastic container should have the numerals 0 − 10 on them. In a large vase have a large collection of plastic flowers. The child places the appropriate number of flowers in each vase.

ACTIVITY: **HOW MANY?**

OBJECTIVE: To provide practice in estimating and counting.

MATERIALS: Jar and small objects, such as: stones, macaroni, buttons, candy.

PROCEDURE: Place a number of objects inside a jar. On the bottom of the jar place a piece of tape on which the correct number of objects is printed. The child then tries to estimate the number of objects that are in the jar. After estimating, the child counts the objects in the jar.

265

ACTIVITY: **FIRST & LAST**

OBJECTIVE: To help the child understand the terms first, last, middle.

MATERIALS: Books or other objects around the house.

PROCEDURE: Place five books in a row. Starting at (child's) left, talk about first. Go on to the end of the row and talk about last. Have the child count in from each side to find the middle. Do this with different objects (always an odd number).

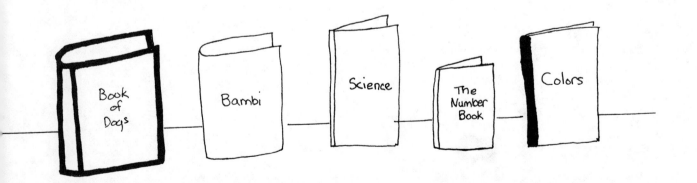

ACTIVITY: **MORE OR LESS?**

OBJECTIVE: To help the child use the terms accurately more, less, few, many.

MATERIALS: Objects at hand (i.e., beans, stones).

PROCEDURE: Make two piles. In one pile place two beans, in the other pile place many beans. Ask which has more? Less? Many? Few?

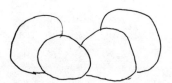

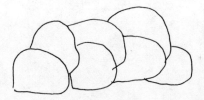

ACTIVITY: **QUANTITY WORDS**

OBJECTIVE: To help the child accurately use the limiting terms of more, less, many, and few.

MATERIALS: Lots of beans, stones, blocks, etc.

PROCEDURE: Make two piles for the child. In one pile, place two items and in the other pile, place many objects. Ask the child to choose the pile with the most in it. Talk about the difference in size or weight in piles.

1) Even piles up more. Ask which has more, less, same. Do it again and make the piles the same. Have the child count the (beans) piles to see they are the same.

2) Have child make a pile (of beans). Have him make another pile of more (beans). Have him make another pile of less (beans). Have him make two piles the same.

3) Have the child make a pile of many (beans). Have him make a pile of a few (beans, more than two).

4) Ask questions about things around you, example:
   *Are there more chairs or tables in this room?
   *Are there more or less doors than windows in this room?
   *Do you have many or just a few shoes?

268

Nearest

ACTIVITY:	**NEARER, NEARER**
OBJECTIVE:	To provide practice with the concept nearer and farther.
MATERIALS:	None.
PROCEDURE:	Begin by determining if the child understands the meaning of the following words: here, there, near, nearer, nearest, far, farther, farthest. These words can be learned and practiced by placing two objects on a table. Place the objects a considerable distance apart and indicate that the objects are far apart, move them close together and indicate they are near. Move the objects and vary the phrases to match the remaining words. After the child demonstrates an understanding of the above words, tell him you're going to play a game. Pick an object that can easily be hidden. Tell the child you will hide it somewhere in the room while he is in another room. Now tell him to leave. Hide the object. When he returns and begins searching for the item, give hints as he moves about. If he is moving nearer to the object, say, "Nearer, nearer." If he starts to move away from the object say, "Farther, farther."

Nearer

Near

Far

Farther

Farthest

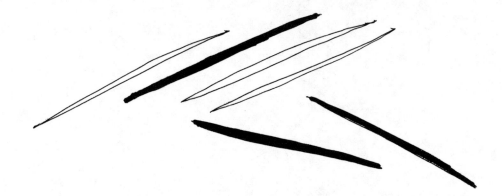

ACTIVITY: **PATTERNS**

OBJECTIVE: To develop awareness of pattern, logical thinking and sequence.

MATERIALS: Colored plastic tooth picks.

PROCEDURE: With your child watching, lay out the tooth picks according to set patterns. The design you make should consist of a regular color pattern repeated over and over. As you lay down the tooth picks, help your child perceive the pattern. After you think he has caught on, ask him, "What comes next?" See if he can select the correct color tooth pick and place it according to the pattern.

VARIATION: Copy Cat. Lay out a tooth pick pattern for your child to copy with his own set of tooth picks.

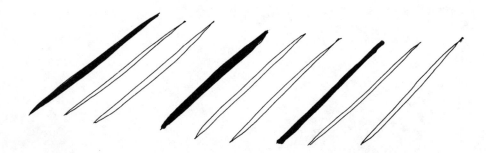

ACTIVITY: **ORGAN PIPES**

OBJECTIVE: To help the child place objects in a height, progressive order.

MATERIALS: Cardboard tubing, scissors.

PROCEDURE: Cut cardboard tubing into 1/2" graduated pieces. The child takes the graduated pieces and experiments until he has the pieces in an orderly, progressive row.

VARIATION: After an orderly row is set up, have the child close his eyes while you remove one piece. Ask the child where the pattern is broken.

ACTIVITY: **BOTTLES AND WATER**

OBJECTIVE: To help the child place objects in a progressive order via increasing amount.

MATERIALS: Ten empty bottles of same size and structure, food coloring, and water.

PROCEDURE: Use 10 empty bottles and add colored water in increasing amounts in each bottle. Put caps on the bottles. The child takes the bottles and lines them up in order.

VARIATION: Discuss most, least. Which bottle has the most water in it? Which has the least?

ACTIVITY: **FLANNEL GROUPING**

OBJECTIVE: To provide practice in sorting shapes and placing the correct numeral with each set.

MATERIALS: Flannelboard, ten patterns of flannel shapes with a varying number of each (1 – 10), flannel numerals.

PROCEDURE: Have the child sort out the ten patterns of flannel shapes into sets and place the correct numeral with each set.

VARIATIONS: 1) The flannel numerals may have dots on the back so that they are self checking.

              2) The entire activity may be done with construction paper shapes and placing the shapes in envelopes labeled 1 – 10.

ART INDEX

GAME INDEX

COOKING INDEX

SCIENCE INDEX

MATH INDEX

NOTES

NOTES

NOTES